Fifty Days with God

Fifty Days with God

A Jubilee

JEFFREY D. JOHNSON

Foreword by Tim Sheranko

WIPF & STOCK · Eugene, Oregon

FIFTY DAYS WITH GOD
A Jubilee

Copyright © 2025 Jeffrey D. Johnson. All rights reserved. Except for brief quotations in critical publications or reviews, no part of this book may be reproduced in any manner without prior written permission from the publisher. Write: Permissions, Wipf and Stock Publishers, 199 W. 8th Ave., Suite 3, Eugene, OR 97401.

Wipf & Stock
An Imprint of Wipf and Stock Publishers
199 W. 8th Ave., Suite 3
Eugene, OR 97401

www.wipfandstock.com

PAPERBACK ISBN: 979-8-3852-3469-1
HARDCOVER ISBN: 979-8-3852-3470-7
EBOOK ISBN: 979-8-3852-3471-4

01/09/25

All Scripture quotations, unless otherwise noted, are taken from the Holy Bible, New King James Version, copyright © 1979, 1980, 1982 by Thomas Nelson, Inc. Used by permission.

For Louise, the one who rescues me!

Contents

Foreword by Tim Sheranko — ix
Prefatory Note — xi
Acknowledgments — xiii
Day 1: What Is God's Kiss? — 1
Day 2: God of Shalom! — 3
Day 3: Seven Ways Psalm 91 Brings Hope, Peace, and Security — 6
Day 4: Adonai Elohim — 9
Day 5: A Holy Hush — 12
Day 6: Encounter with God — 15
Day 7: Broken Pieces, Leaven Bread, and Shavuot — 18
Day 8: "Do-Over" — 21
Day 9: Climbing the Wall — 24
Day 10: Arriving Early! — 28
Day 11: God Chose — 30
Day 12: Hallel: Psalms 113–118 — 34
Day 13: The Heart of Worship During Challenging Times! — 36
Day 14: Jerusalem — 38
Day 15: Here I Am! — 41
Day 16: Puff of Air — 44
Day 17: Waiting! — 46
Day 18: Waking Up! — 48
Day 19: A Mother's Plea! — 50
Day 20: A Mother's Concern! — 52
Day 21: Image of God! — 55

CONTENTS

Day 22: Ancient Words	57
Day 23: Long Nose!	61
Day 24: Deep Waters	64
Day 25: Jesus Received Worship	66
Day 26: Love First Mentioned!	68
Day 27: The Fifth Directive!	71
Day 28: You Will Know!	73
Day 29: Women with "Fire"!	74
Day 30: Raising Hands!	77
Day 31: Charity, Duty, Love!	80
Day 32: Mysterious Disasters—The Ninth Day of Av!	82
Day 33: Don't Mess with Abraham	85
Day 34: Problems and Solutions—From the Prophet Haggai!	88
Day 35: Fear: *Yir'ah*	91
Day 36: Your Name	93
Day 37: Messed Up!	96
Day 38: Does God Care?	98
Day 39: Grandma's Prayer	101
Day 40: God Declares	105
Day 41: Yes Be Yes!	108
Day 42: Six Things to Remember About God's Silence	110
Day 43: Your Work Continues!	112
Day 44: Mystery of the Olive Tree	115
Day 45: The One Worthy	117
Day 46: The Right Thing to Do!	120
Day 47: Very Personal	123
Day 48: Scars and Circumstances	125
Day 49: Discovering Your Purpose, *Shema*!	128
Day 50: The Anchor	130
About Dr. Jeff	133
Bibliography	135
Subject Index	137
Scripture Index	141

Foreword

In a world filled with much uncertainty and turmoil we can find much-needed hope. The source of our security is seen all throughout Scripture. Psalm 62:5–8 states,

> My soul, wait silently for God alone,
> For my expectation *is* from Him.
> He only *is* my rock and my salvation;
> *He is* my defense;
> I shall not be moved.
> In God *is* my salvation and my glory;
> The rock of my strength,
> *And* my refuge, *is* in God.
> Trust in Him at all times, you people;
> Pour out your heart before Him;
> God *is* a refuge for us. *Selah*

David was experiencing a difficult time with the rebellion of his son Absalom. In running for his own life, his attitude was one of determination to stand strong believing God would be his defense and that he would not be moved. The psalmist truly declares that all honor and victory comes from Almighty God alone. God is sovereign, steadfast, and faithful.

Time and time again, he offers his people a place of refuge and is a safe haven even in troublesome times. Just as we see in David's life, "a man after God's own heart," God continues to use ordinary people for extraordinary tasks to fulfill his purpose.

It truly is an honor knowing and working with Dr. Jeff and Israel Today Ministries from the very beginning. We have seen

FOREWORD

God's hand at work where ITM is being used on the front lines blessing God's ancient people of Israel. ITM is dedicated and has never ceased, even in global hardships, to provide meals, resources, and support to children, orphanages, and holocaust survivors in Israel. The international relationships that have been established are a result of Dr. Jeff's passion to "fulfill the Abrahamic covenant," which has been manifested in practical and profound ways.

In *Fifty Days with God*, Dr. Jeff paves the way for believers from all over the world to experience encounters with Yeshua, the Son of God. This devotional reflects Dr. Jeff's passion and love for God and heart for the Jewish people, as well as his desire to teach and educate believers to know in a deeper way the customs and traditions of God's chosen people, Israel, and God's unconditional love for his people in the body of Messiah Jesus.

Hearts will be challenged each day to embrace the truth of the gospel and be encouraged to faithfully follow and passionately "love the Lord your God with all your heart, with all your soul, and with all your strength" (Deut 6:4).

Anyone who is experiencing challenging times of uncertainty or great pain and turmoil can be assured that God's word will bring peace. Philippians 4:5–7 declares, "Let your gentleness be known to all men. The Lord is at hand. Be anxious for nothing, but in everything by prayer and supplication, with thanksgiving, let your requests be made known to God; and the peace of God, which surpasses all understanding, will guard your hearts and minds through Christ Jesus."

May God use *Fifty Days with God* in your life, in a very intimate and reflective way, as you take time each day to seek him.

Rev. Tim Sheranko
Executive Pastor, First Baptist Church/East Longmeadow, MA; Israel Today Ministries' Board Corporate Secretary/Treasurer

Prefatory Note

Why fifty? In Scripture, the Jubilee is a year of release, rest, and forgiveness which occurs every fifty years, after seven Sabbath years (Lev 25). The word "jubilee" comes from the Hebrew word "yobel," which means "ram's horn." The Jubilee was marked by the blowing of a ram's horn trumpet to signal the beginning of the year. So, therefore, the number fifty represents a release from debts and burdens, a freedom and a new start.

In a day of great uncertainty and anxiety, *Fifty Days with God: A Jubilee* provides courage and assurance for the believer who is struggling with holding onto faith. Considering Hebrew meaning and nuance to poignant chapters and stories found in Holy Scripture brings a fresh wind of hope. When facing deep waters, this book highlights solutions to the challenges facing the follower of the Messiah Jesus. As we journey on the path of faith, *Fifty Days with God* guides the disciple, pointing to principles and values found within Scripture. This book will strengthen, encourage, and remind the believer that when the sun comes up in the morning, we get to have a "do-over" (Lam 3). We can reset, rest, and return home. This is our Jubilee!

Shalom and Blessings,
Until He comes, we are
Together Under His Wings,

Jeffrey D. Johnson
2024

Acknowledgments

The messages in this book were prepared during many weeks and months of a very busy and active ministry. They are not for scholars and exegetes, but for regular followers of Messiah Jesus. However, pastors, Bible teachers, and scholars will find this volume very helpful in teaching Scripture.

No claim is made for originality, but the writer is deeply grateful for the help he received from many sources, including those in the bibliography.

DAY 1

What Is God's Kiss?

Let him kiss me with the kisses of his mouth—For your love is better than wine. —Song 1:2

The Shulamite desires close contact with her lover. Kissing is not done at a distance. She is not satisfied with a distant relationship. Kissing only occurs in close, face-to-face relationships.

The Scriptures tells us that God spoke to Moses *"p'anim al p'anim"—face to face*. The Lord spoke to Moses face to face, as a man speaks to his friend (Exod 33:11).

The writer of Hebrews states that "God, who at various times and in various ways spoke in time past to the fathers by the prophets, has in these last days spoken to us by His Son, whom He has appointed heir of all things, through whom also He made the worlds" (Heb 1:1, 2).

What exactly is a kiss from God? According to Jewish tradition, it is a living word of prophecy. In the Christian context, have you ever had the experience of reading or hearing something from the Bible which suddenly came alive to you? Literally jumping off the page, and you knew that God was speaking to *you*? If you have experienced this, you have been kissed by God!

There's nothing quite like having direct contact with the Creator through his word. This is the epitome of all communication. This is what we were created for: to have communion with God.

We yearn for this direct communion with God, in the same way that pious Jews yearned for the coming of Messiah.

Jews awaited his coming and his kiss. The psalmist wrote, "Kiss the Son, Blessed are all those who put their trust in Him" (Ps 2:12). Jewish scholars often quote Deut 18:18 when commenting on the kisses of God: "I will raise up for them a Prophet like you from among their brethren, and will put My words in His mouth, and He shall speak to them all that I command Him."

They conclude that the phrase "kisses of God" refer to prophecy, or speaking his word. "Thus saith the Lord!"

In his profound sermon in the temple in Acts 3, Peter stated that "this Prophet, who should come spoken here in Deuteronomy, is none other than Jesus of Nazareth" (Deut 18:15, 19). He is the living Word.

We long to hear from God—to be, if you will, "kissed" by him. It is his desire to embrace you and to kiss you as many times as you will receive.

The Lord's kisses are life-giving. Quoting Deut 8:3, Jesus said, "Man shall not live by bread alone; but man lives by every word that proceeds from the mouth of the Lord." In other words, we live by kisses from God.

How do I receive a kiss from God? Go to his word. Read God's word with a sense of expectancy, a desire to be kissed, and have great confidence in the promise from John 10:27: "My sheep hear my voice and I know them and they follow me."

The idea is this: if you are a child of God, you are part of the "bride of Christ." When you go to your prayer closet (the bridal chamber), with Bible in hand, look up into the face of Jesus, our heavenly bridegroom, and say, "You may kiss the bride!"

To learn more about the Song of Songs, read Dr. Jeff's book, *Song of Songs, the Greatest Lover* (Wipf & Stock Publishers, 2020).

DAY 2

God of Shalom!

GOD OF GODS (HEB. *ELOHAY ELOHIM*)

> For the Lord your God is God of gods and Lord of lords, the great God, mighty and awesome. —Deut 10:17

There are other "gods" but our God is greater than all of them. This "God of gods" thinks about us. You are on his mind: "But I am poor and needy; *Yet* the Lord thinks upon me" (Ps 40:17).

God thinks about you and me. This gives me immeasurable comfort. *This "great God" is thinking about me, and he is thinking about you!*

GOD OF SHALOM (HEB. *ELOHAY HA-SHALOM*)

> And the God of peace will crush Satan under your feet shortly. The grace of our Lord Jesus Christ be with you. Amen. (Rom 16:20)

Similarly, as Moses mentioned above, Paul tells us that *God is greater*, greater than Satan. The word "peace" that Paul uses is the Hebrew word "shalom."

"Shalom" means more than just peace. When we think of peace, we may think of a stress-free day or a sunset or seeing the stars at night that make us feel a certain way.

The root of "shalom" is connected to Hebrew verbs that mean "to fulfill that which is lacking, to fill a void" or "make a payment."

We recall Jesus appearing to the disciples after the resurrection saying, "Peace to you" (John 20:21); in the Hebrew it is *shalom aleichem*, meaning "peace be with you."

Jesus was saying, "Your void, emptiness, or lack no longer exists; I've paid the bill on your behalf; your sin is forgiven; the hole in your heart is now filled with my mercy and love."

If "shalom" meant this alone, that would be enough! However, there is even more to the word "peace." "Shalom" in ancient Jewish tradition has the idea of being completely unified with God and others. In fact, being unified with God and others was more important than proving one's view of truth. Now this may make some of us uncomfortable as we have been taught to defend the truth.

The idea here does not take away from a believer defending the truth verbally as such with a polemic or apologetics. The thought of the ancient Jewish mind is that *you* are more important than my view, and that being unified with God and/or others outweighs any denominational expectations.

Early believers taught that those who love God should love and pursue peace with him and that they should love their neighbors, enticing them toward the Scriptures.

A New Testament principle of enticing would be *provocation*: "For I speak to you Gentiles; inasmuch as I am an apostle to the Gentiles, I magnify my ministry, if by any means I may provoke to jealousy those who are my flesh and save some of them" (Rom 11:13, 14).

This is exactly how I came to know the Lord personally. The church basically loved me into the kingdom with their peaceful love for God and others. There were no arguments as to what is truth. They did answer my questions, but not in an argumentative way. They simply loved me and accepted me in my dreadful state.

Their peaceful love for God and me resulted in me being enticed toward the Scriptures.

I didn't know it at the time, but I know now that it was God the Holy Spirit who was drawing me to Jesus. God used the peaceful spirit of these church members to soften my stone-heart, and as a result, they were free to share the Scriptures with me

May our lives exhibit peace, enticing people to the truth that Jesus is the "God of gods" and the "God of shalom." Our daily challenge and joy is to pursue peace with God and others (our neighbors) which results in attracting people to the truth.

DAY 3

Seven Ways Psalm 91 Brings Hope, Peace, and Security

There is no shortage of fear, anger, and anxiety in the world right now. But reading and understanding Ps 91, one of the most read and relied upon of all the psalms, brings us hope, peace, and security.

Here are seven ways the mercy of God's protection, provision, and power are brought to light with clarity through Ps 91:

There are many voices today saying "come to Jesus and all will be well." Yet, Scripture teaches that in the world we will have tribulation and testing. Jesus said, "Count the cost." Psalm 91 gives us God's strategy of hope when testing, trials, sicknesses, and evil attacks come calling.

Psalm 91 speaks of God's protection from dangers and things like plagues. The Talmud (the central text of Rabbinic Judaism) refers to Ps 91 as the "Song of Plagues" (Shev Shema'tata 15b). The psalm reminds us that believers are in the "shade" of the Almighty. We are protected from harm and from anything or anyone pursuing us. God will never abandon his children. There is no need to fear; he will help us (Heb 13:5–6; Isa 41:13).

The psalm addresses the sovereignty of God, the ruler of the universe. Believers are under the divine presence of God. God's protection is an encompassing shield.

The temple, where the presence of God dwells, is where you find safety and peace. For those of you who are believers in Jesus, remember Paul's words: "Your body is the temple of the Holy Spirit who is in you, whom you have from God, and you are not your own. . . . For you were bought at a price; therefore, glorify God in your body and in your spirit, which are God's" (1 Cor 6:19–20). The peace, protection, and safety we all long for is found in Jesus. The presence of God, through the Holy Spirit, dwells in you. We need not fear.

Reading Ps 91, we learn our divine bodyguards (angels) fight for us. Our angels have intimate conversations with God. As we journey with God and trials come, even when we do not have immediate answers, we must persevere and keep walking until the answer comes.

The psalm reminds us to develop a sense of awe, reverence, and expectancy for the Lord's presence. There is no pretentiousness here, no artificial posturing. A developed sense of spiritual intuition acknowledges the Lord is in our midst.

Abraham recognized the angels and the Lord who visited him in Gen 18. His acts of humility, reverence, washing feet, and serving them is a mirror of what Jesus taught his disciples (John 13; Matt 20:28). In times of trial or healing through pain, we are to serve and worship God. It's not about us; it's about him. As with Sarah, who laughed when told she was to have a child, God knows our hearts and how we often teeter toward questioning what he says. When pushed, we deny that we "laughed." Fear of the unknown often causes us to recoil. But then, lo and behold, the miraculous happens. God can do the impossible!

God does not keep us free from trouble. When trouble comes, he gives us choices to make. The psalmist chose to make the "Most High" his refuge. We have a choice to run towards or run away from God during times of trial. Our plans, our schemes, our strengths, and our failures are some of the things that seemingly would put a wedge between us and God, but nothing can separate us from his love (Rom 8:35–39). Like David, we always can reach out to God who loves us and seek refuge in his haven so that we do not wander away from his path.

Life without hardships and testing is impossible, whether in the flesh or the spirit. God has given each of us free will. We choose. Virtue, strength, and wisdom physically and spiritually are acquired. We must discipline both body and spirit.

Resistance, testing, and difficulty strengthen both the body and the spirit, and all of us will experience these difficulties. When the enemy comes, remember the words of our Master: "These things I have spoken to you, that in Me you may have peace. In the world you will have tribulation; but be of good cheer, I have overcome the world" (John 16:33). Holiness, security, and peace unfolds as we trust in the protection and truth of the "Most High."

DAY 4

Adonai Elohim

Moses penned the sacred words of the creation story with great specificity in the book of Genesis.

CHAPTER 1

In chapter 1 of Genesis, you will find phrases such as "in the beginning God created the heavens and the earth," "then God said," "and God saw," "God called," and "so God created."

CHAPTER 2

By the time we arrive in chapter 2, you will find that Moses changes his emphasis: "And the Lord God formed man"; "The Lord God planted"; "The Lord God said"; "The Lord God caused"; "The Lord God called."

Do you see the difference? In chapter 1, Moses penned the word "Elohim," translated in English as "God." "Elohim" describes God as the sovereign architect of creation, the judge, or the one who decides and determines. The emphasis that Elohim, the sovereign judge, who created and called, the one who determined and had set things in order, was changed.

The Change

In chapter 2, Moses changes it up for a very important reason. He uses the words "YHVH Elohim," or as it is in English, "Lord God." YHVH is called the "Tetragrammaton," which is the transliteration in four letters of the unspeakable name of God.

The Name

Jews will not attempt to speak nor write the unspeakable name of God. They will say "HaShem," which means "The Name," or "Adonai," which means "Lord." When writing the unspeakable name of God, Jews will write "G-d," "L-rd," "HaShem," or "Adonai."

Mercy

YHVH emphasizes the mercy of God. Why was Moses highlighting the concept of a "merciful judge" in chapter 2? Because man was being created. The pinnacle of creation was about to happen—man and woman.

The sovereign, all-knowing Judge knew that man and woman would need mercy; indeed, mercy was given as God was first to shed blood in Gen 3, and finally at Calvary, to cover and forgive their sin.

The Covenant

In the Middle East, when you are a guest in someone's home, there is an unspoken covenant between you and that family. As a guest, you are considered family, in which they will protect you, shelter you, and feed you; they would risk their lives for you. I first learned of this unspoken covenant some fifteen years ago when I was hosted by a Palestinian Christian family and terrorist activity was prevalent. I felt safe and loved.

Hiding Place

So, it is with YHVH. This is what is being said in the Psalms:

> But the Lord [YHVH] has been my defense, and my God [Elohim] the rock of my refuge. (Ps 94:22)
>
> I will love You, O Lord [YHVH], my strength. The Lord [YHVH] is my rock and my fortress and my deliverer; My God [EL(ohim)], my strength, in whom I will trust; My shield and the horn of my salvation, my stronghold. (Ps 18:1–2)
>
> You are my hiding place; You shall preserve me from trouble; You shall surround me with songs of deliverance. *Selah.* (Ps 32:7)

The "merciful God," "Adonai Elohim," provides provision, protection, a place of refuge, shelter, a hiding place, and forgiveness. He is our dwelling place, our tent, our covering, our Savior.

DAY 5

A Holy Hush

Once again, I marveled and praised God for the authentic worship within our Jerusalem congregation—a congregation principally attended by Jewish believers along with a few believing gentiles.

HOLY WORSHIP—DIFFERENT LANGUAGES

Not long ago, before the pandemic came upon us, we had visitors from a tour group worship with us. People were from Asia and Europe. Everyone in the worship service knew "Turn Your Eyes Upon Jesus." Both Jews and Gentiles sang in their respective languages of Hebrew, English, Korean, and German. What a holy, beautiful sound it was—a glimpse of heaven.

HOLY WORDS

Scripture was etched upon the ark (where the Torah scroll is placed) and the bema (pulpit). Our beloved shepherd-teacher Yossi (he does not refer to himself as "Rabbi") led us in psalms, hymns, and Israeli spiritual songs, as well as many prayers and Jewish blessings. He read Scripture from the Torah (five books of Moses), Nevi'im (Prophets), Gospels, and Epistles, followed by a responsive reading from the Psalms (K'tuvim). He then sat (a very rabbinical thing to do) and taught the sermon.

HOLY REMEMBRANCE

Communion was then observed toward the end of the service. With approximately twenty-five people in attendance on a regular Shabbat, the service produces a very intimate experience. The congregation stood in a semicircle and Yossi broke off a piece from the large unleavened matzah bread, giving it to each person and saying their name, along with "this is the body of Messiah, broken for you." He prayed, then we all partook. The wine was then poured in a similar fashion, given to each person, and again, he said their name, along with "this is the blood of Messiah, the Lamb of God, *Yeshua HaMashiach*, who shed his blood for the forgiveness of sins." He prayed, then together we partook.

It was gently communicated that communion was for baptized believers only; therefore, some people reverently sat in their seats, not partaking for whatever personal reason, wiping their tears from their eyes as the holiness and presence of God was profoundly realized.

HOLY HUSH

There was a simplicity, a reverence, a devoutness, a devotion—a "holy hush"—that hovered over the three-hour worship service. The last part of the worship was the blessing over the children. All the children came forward and stood under Yossi's tallit (prayer shawl). He prayed the Aaronic blessing over them: "The Lord bless you and keep you; the Lord make His face shine upon you, and be gracious to you; the Lord lift up His countenance upon you, and give you peace" (Num 6:24–26).

HOLY LOVE

And then a few final words, another blessing over the congregation, followed by Oneg, which is a time of gathering together with food, singing, study, discussion, and socializing. It was a good day of worship!

DAY 6

Encounter with God

Recently, a group of people joined me in the Holy Land. At each location, we walked, talked, and read Scripture. The Scripture was a record of the events regarding the places and spaces we walked. They heard the sounds, smelled the air, touched the stone, tasted the food, and saw with their own eyes where Jesus walked and where the prophets lived. All their senses were engaged, and the reality of God's presence was powerful.

They experienced God on a level never realized before. Tears flowed freely, their exhilaration elevated to new heights, and their souls soared towards heaven as they journeyed together in God's presence. Like the prophets of old, each one had an encounter with God.

JEREMIAH

> Then the LORD put forth His hand and touched my mouth, and the LORD said to me: "Behold I have put My words in your mouth." (Jer 1:9)

One should take note that here the hand of God is sent to touch the prophet's mouth. God put his "words in" Jeremiah's mouth.

ISAIAH

Isaiah had a similar encounter with God, and yet, it was very different: "Then one of the seraphim flew to me, having in his hand a live coal which he had taken with the tongs from the altar and he touched my mouth with it and said, 'Behold, this has touched your lips; Your iniquity is taken away, and your sin purged'" (Isa 6:6, 7).

Being an older man, Isaiah had admitted he was a man of unclean lips—having a lifetime of flaws, living in a generation of immorality.

Therefore, the seraphim took the tongs and grabbed a searing hot coal from the altar and touched his mouth, thus purifying and forgiving his sin and releasing him from the guilt of his sin. This was a very powerful, life-changing moment.

Similarly, Jeremiah, though being a younger man, had experienced the hand of God, not to take away his sins, but rather to give him the ability to speak God's word—also a powerful, life-changing moment.

EZEKIEL

Ezekiel swallowed a scroll that tasted like honey, filling him with sacred mysteries and truths to empower him to speak to Israel (Ezek 3).

WHAT IS NECESSARY FOR YOU?

All three men had an encounter with God. All three men had a life-changing experience to the actual degree of their personal need.

The older Isaiah needed forgiveness—which requires an intensity of burning transparency.

The younger Jeremiah needed courage—therefore, God revealed his "hand" to the prophet. He saw something familiar that looked like a human hand; as a result, Jeremiah would not retreat nor be frightened. Instead, Jeremiah was empowered, and he advanced the message of God.

Ezekiel, the mystical sage, ate the scroll of mysteries and truths. The honeycombed scroll gave the prophet energy to proclaim deep, prophetic veracities to Israel.

Simply, God meets you where you are, and gives you what is necessary to address life's challenges that are before you at this moment. Do not be afraid, and be of good cheer—God will give you exactly what is needed for the moment.

DAY 7

Broken Pieces, Leaven Bread, and Shavuot

MOSES

Shavuot, or Pentecost, memorializes Moses's ascent up Sinai where he met with God to receive the Decalogue (the Ten Commandments) written on two stone tablets by God himself, the Torah, and instruction regarding building the tabernacle. He was there for forty days and nights (Exod 19–32; Deut 9:9–11).

As Moses came down the mountain, he saw the Israelites backslide into paganism and idolatry worshiping a golden calf. In his anger, Moses smashed the tablets of the Ten Commandments into bits and pieces, shards flying everywhere (Exod 32:19, 20).

Early the next day, Moses ascended back up the mountain for another forty days to plead for atonement for the people, begging for mercy for their disobedience (Exod 32:30, 34; Deut 9:25).

Moses ascended a third time on Sinai for another forty days and nights (Exod 34:2, 28). The Lord, acting upon Moses's plea not to destroy the people, told him to make an ark of wood and to cut out two more tablets. God rewrote the commands on the stone and Moses was to put the tablets into the ark of wood (Deut 10:1–5). Moses came down the mountain with the renewed covenant;

BROKEN PIECES, LEAVEN BREAD, AND SHAVUOT

rabbis say the day he came down the mountain was Yom Kippur, the Day of Atonement. Moses was on the mountain a total of 120 days, from Shavuot to Yom Kippur.

PETER

Shavuot (Pentecost) is also the day when the Holy Spirit (*Ruach HaKodesh*) descended upon the 120 in the upper room some 1500 years later, birthing and empowering the church (Acts 2).

On that day, the Holy Spirit came upon each of them as rushing wind and tongues of fire, and they began to speak in tongues (languages). People in the area that heard this strange noise were curious and began to gather around. Peter, raising his voice, began to preach about the prophets and lead them to the message of the gospel. Over three thousand came to faith in Jesus.

BROKEN PIECES

What happened to the broken shards, bits, and pieces of stone from the original two tablets? The instructions written by the finger of God are now shattered. What would you do with them? Step on them? Spread them around? Ignore them? What?

Jewish tradition tells us that the second tablets, along with the broken tablets, were placed in the ark made of beaten gold (Talmud, Bava Batra 14b). But why keep the broken pieces? Aren't they a symbol of disobedience and punishment? Why remind us of our disobedience?

LEAVENED BREAD

During Shavuot (Pentecost), leavened bread is used in the festivities. Leaven is the yeast that makes the bread rise. Leaven is a type of sin in the Bible. In contrast, during Passover, unleavened bread is used to remind us that the lamb is unblemished: the Lamb of God is sinless. The shattering of the two tablets and the leavened bread on Shavuot reminds us that the church is a gathering of shattered, broken people who found mercy, healing, and forgiveness through Messiah Jesus.

POINTS TO PONDER

1. The shards of stone and unleavened bread, though symbols of disobedience and sin, remind us of God's grace.
2. God showed mercy to the people and created a second set of tablets, and Jesus forgave our sin, becoming our atoning sacrifice (1 John 2:2).
3. God took the broken bits and pieces of our life and gave us hope (Eph 2:1–14).
4. Being reminded of our past engenders a motivation to praise God for his mercy and forgiveness.

DAY 8

"Do-Over"

> *Whoever saves a life, it is considered as if he saved an entire world.* —Mishnah Sanhedrin 4:5; Yerushalmi Talmud 4:9

Jewish sages emphasize the importance of a humanity. They understand that every life is precious and valuable, as the Talmud verse above explains. Moses records for us the miracle and mystery of Eden's dust in the creation of Adam on the sixth day.

GENESIS 1:1-25

When God created during the first five days, he said, "Let there be!" (Heb. *yehi*). Grammatically, the Hebrew "Let there be" expresses encouragement or exhortation. In other words, with great joy God urged the creation of the heavens and the earth through his spoken word as the heavens declared his glory (Ps 19:1).

GENESIS 2:7

By the time we arrive on the "sixth day," a profound change happened. "Let us make" is one Hebrew word, *naaseh*, which expresses a command. A directive was spoken, a demand was given. With great divine power and purpose, God was about to do something extraordinary—create humankind in his ["our"] own image (Gen 1:26). The Hebrew word *betzalmeinu* translated "in our image" refers to the original image or imitation.

EDEN'S DUST

God spoke during the first five days, and things came into existence. However, God did not speak man into being; he, with his own hands, as it were, created Adam from the dust of the garden of Eden (Gen 2:7).

With great consideration, calculation, and forethought, Adam was brought into being. The involvement of divine providence and wisdom is beyond comprehension.

FREE WILL

Every human being is stamped with the image of God. Every human being has free will. Every human being has the free will to come to the Father through Jesus or reject the prompting of God. This is a mystery. We all have choices.

People do make wrong decisions during times of fear and uncertainty—even Christians. As believers, we must anchor our minds and actions upon God's word. There are days we do this better. The good news is that when we err, tomorrow God's mercies are renewed (Lam 3). We get to have a "do-over."

In a time of testing, remember God created you in his image. You are no mistake—God makes no mistakes!

POINTS TO PONDER

1. With great divine power and purpose God created you (Ps 139:13–17).

2. With God's own hands he created Adam from Eden's dust.

3. You are stamped with the image of God (Gen 1:17).

"DO-OVER"

4. God thinks about you (Ps 40:17).
5. God will hold your hand, walk with you, and help you (Isa 41:13).
6. If you err, you can begin again.

There are days we do this better. There are days we make right choices and there are days we do not make the right choices. The good news is that when we err, tomorrow God's mercies are renewed. *His mercies never end.*

> They are new every morning; Great is Your faithfulness!
> (Lam 3:22, 23)

We get to have a "do-over." A "do-over" is when we are able to start all over and begin again. God, in his mercy, gives us the opportunity every morning to begin anew, to have a "do-over"—you matter!

DAY 9

Climbing the Wall

A typical Israeli morning was unfolding as Louise and I were planning to go to Bethany, the home of Mary and Martha and the place where Jesus raised Lazarus from the dead.

110-DEGREE HEAT

Ramone was to be our guide. He is a trusted friend who watches over Louise and me (especially me) to keep us safe and out of trouble. In the past, he waited three hours in the hot Jericho desert for me and a dear friend to cross the border from Jordan. At that time, my bag was stolen at the border crossing. I asked Israeli soldiers for assistance. They promptly escorted me back to the Palestinian security area to look for my belongings. It was like the parting of the Red Sea. Once the Palestinian soldiers saw the five Israeli soldiers and this six-foot-two American, they yielded and allowed me to look for my stuff. Unfortunately, we could not find my bag. Nevertheless, Ramone did not know what was going on and faithfully waited in the 110-degree heat until my friend and I appeared. He was somewhat dehydrated, anxious, and very relieved to see us. He was a sight to behold, and I was thankful he stayed the course and waited for us in the desert sun. He is that kind of faithful brother.

CLIMBING THE WALL

Now back to the story. Ramone picked Louise and me up, after which we made a few contacts and completed a few contacts and completed some busy work and then up to the Mount of Olives.

BLOCKED BY THE WALL

As you may know, Israel is erecting a security fence that will separated Israel from a future Palestine. The wall is not to keep people out; rather, it's meant to direct people to go through checkpoints. This will aid Israel in stopping the bad guys from blowing up innocent bystanders shopping at the market or riding a bus.

The road leading to our destination ended up being blocked by the wall. This wall is around twenty-five feet tall and about eighteen inches thick. We could either drive another hour and a half around the mountain and wall or climb over the wall.

Where we were standing, the wall ended, but it was adjoined by another five-foot wall making a "T" shape. This five-foot wall went into the city of Bethany. The options were to climb over this five foot section or to drive around. Well you've guessed it. I looked at Louise and said, "Do you love me?" She said, "Let's do it!"

"DO YOU LOVE ME?"

Oh, did I tell you there were Israeli soldiers guarding this section of the wall? We greeted the soldiers with a sheepish smile. Ramone was standing watch over the car. He said, "I will pray for you." That was somewhat comforting. Did I mention I am not twenty-five anymore? So, I began to climb the wall, holding onto the larger security wall so I would not fall backwards onto the sharp stones below. I stood on top of the five-foot connecting wall, holding onto the large security wall which towered above the smaller wall. I reached down and pulled Louise up. As she stood atop the smaller wall, holding onto the larger, I stepped down to the other side. Then reaching up to grab her hand, Louise shimmied down and was now with me on the other side of the security fence, no longer under the protection of Israeli forces.

MUSLIM JIHADISTS

We turned around only to be greeted by Jihad representatives with AK-47 rifles. Fortunately, there was a barrage of press taking photos of us climbing over the wall. We swiftly passed through the soldiers and press to go on our way. Whew! By the way, if you see a photo on the internet of two people climbing over a wall in the Middle East, yes, it is really Louise and me.

We walked for some time through the village of Bethany until we found the tomb of Lazarus (this was before it became a tourist destination, now being well-lit and easily accessible). The villagers were friendly and very helpful. Some were amazed that we were there walking through the streets. Being in the Holy Land is the ultimate contradiction. It is the most volatile chunk of real estate on the planet, and yet, it is the most peaceful, spiritually refreshing place to experience.

We literally journeyed down through a tunnel and crawled into the tomb and were silenced by the miracle that unfolded here two thousand years ago. To be reminded of the resurrection and assurance of eternal life in Messiah Jesus was priceless. And yet, our hearts were reminded also of the millions of Jews and Arabs who do not know of God's redeeming grace through his Son, the Lord Jesus.

Oh, by the way, we had to repeat the process to find our way back to Ramone, who once again was patiently waiting for us to return. As the sun was beginning to set, Louise and I were climbing back over the wall. Would we do it again? Yep!

COUNTING THE COST

To follow Jesus requires counting the cost. We all are on a journey, whether we are patiently waiting, climbing, crawling, or simply standing in silence. God provides what is needed at the exact moment. His grace is sufficient for today. He will also take care of tomorrow.

God is in control of everything that takes place in our lives. His purpose will be fulfilled no matter how bleak it may look, no matter how challenging it may seem. "Then Job answered the Lord and said: 'I know You can do everything, and that no purpose of Yours can be withheld from You'" (Job 42:1–2).

DAY 10

Arriving Early!

O God, You are my God; Early will I seek You; My soul thirst for You; My flesh longs for You in a dry and thirsty land where there is no water. So, I have looked for You in the sanctuary, to see Your power and Your glory. Because Your lovingkindness is better than life, my lips shall praise You. —Ps 63:1–3

"Early will I seek you." With great intensity, I yearn for you. When I wake, you are the first one on my mind. When a person loves God, he seeks him constantly. It is a passion that is not an intellectual assent; rather, it is a passion that is an experiential anticipation and craving. Like Peter stated with great pathos, we "were eyewitnesses of His majesty. . . . And we heard this voice which came from heaven when we were with Him on the holy mountain" (2 Pet 1:16, 18). As a result, Peter said, we know "that no prophecy of Scripture is of any private interpretation, but holy men of God spoke as they were moved by the Holy Spirit" (2 Pet 1:20–21) In other words, we were there. We experienced for ourselves the presence of God. So it is with those who seek God early.

The Hebrew word for "early" is *shachar* and means "black," such as in the dawn. The Talmud emphasizes that when you seek God early, you discover the hidden mysteries and secrets from him.

ARRIVING EARLY!

When I was an adjunct professor, at times a student would arrive early before the others with questions about life and theology. In those moments, casual conversations unfolded between the student and myself—intellectual capacity for the student becomes more personal. In contrast, when the class began, I would speak in an official manner—in a more formal way that is communal and less personal, relating to all the students collectively. So it is with God. When you seek him "early," *you will discover holy things that will impact your soul and mind on a very personal level.*

The rabbis share a principle that whosoever shows up earliest in the sanctuary, before others, unites himself to the Shekinah (the presence of God) in a personal union. Arriving early does not imply a time; rather, the implication is that you passionately love him and desire to worship and know him, and that he is first in your life.

When arriving "early" you may find God "high and lifted up" as Isaiah did in the temple, saying, "Woe is me for my eyes have seen" God (Isa 6:1, 5). Or, like Peter, you may be able to say with confidence, "I know, I believe, I trust, and I experienced His presence" (2 Pet 1:16–21). Or, like David, you may be able to say, "I have looked for God in the sanctuary, and saw His power and glory—therefore, my lips shall praise Him" (Ps 63:2–3).

Solomon penned the words this way regarding God: "I love those who love me, and those who seek me diligently (early) will find me" (Prov 8:17).

The Hebrew word "love" is *ahav*, meaning "I will give." When you love someone, your focus is on them, not yourself. "I will give": What does God give? "Those who seek me early shall find me." The word "find" is the Hebrew word *matsa*, meaning "to acquire." In other words, when you seek him early, he will enable you to discover, or "acquire," profound mysteries found only in God—through his word. Seek him early and God will fill your heart with his power and glory.

DAY 11

God Chose

And He said, "Your name shall no longer be called Jacob, but Israel; for you have struggled with God and with men, and have prevailed." —Gen 32:28

Before the world was created, and before the stars danced in majestic design; before the galaxies displayed their glorious splendor, and before Adam and Eve graced the landscape of our blue-jeweled-planet; before there was light or darkness, and before anything was realized; before time itself, there was God.

Within the eternal mind of God, before anything was created in heaven or on earth, visible, or, invisible, there was a plan, there was a design, and a purpose that he set in motion.

You see, he is before all things, and in him all things consist. And Christ is the head of the body, the church, who is the beginning, the firstborn from the dead, that in all things he may have the preeminence (Col 2).

God chose to communicate through his creation. David said, "The Heavens declare the glory of God and the firmament shows His handiwork" (Ps 19:1). Just by simply looking up into the heavens, you know that God exists and is there.

God chose to communicate through his word. The psalmist wrote, "Forever, O Lord, your word is settled in heaven. Your faithfulness endures to all generations; you established the earth and it abides" (Ps 119:89-90*)*. David stated, "You have magnified your word above all your name" (Ps 138:2*)*.

God chose to communicate through a nomadic people. Nearly four thousand years ago, God chose a seventy-five-year-old man from Mesopotamia and made a covenant with him. Abraham lived some three hundred years after the flood, and Jewish tradition declares that his mother took him as a child to learn from Noah and Shem as they were still alive during his lifetime.

God chose to make a covenant with Abraham (Gen 12:1-3). When the Lord made this covenant, he began to communicate specifically through a chosen people. These tribes were the descendants of Abraham and Sarah. Through Abraham came the promised son Isaac. Then Jacob was born, then the twelve sons of Jacob, the patriarchs, followed by Moses, the prophets, judges, and kings.

God chose to convey a story through these descendants of Abraham, a story so wonderful, so profound, so simple, and yet so complex. It was a story of an anointed one who would come, a messiah who would redeem Israel and deliver them from their oppressors. This messiah would be the glory of Israel and a light to the gentile.

God chose to reveal a promise concerning land that exclusively belonged to the descendants of Isaac, Abraham's son. This hope touched the very soul within the children of Israel. This promised piece of real estate is at the heart of the tension throughout the Middle East. Who owns the land is the main issue that is so provocative that people are willing to give their lives for this portion of property.

GOD CHOSE BORDERS OF HIS CHOSEN LAND

Genesis 15:18 describes the land area from the river of Egypt to the Euphrates. This is in part the same location as Israel today. Israel does not have all the land promised her. The fulfillment of all the land is yet to come.

GOD CHOSE DESCENDANTS TO DWELL IN THIS LAND

God chose the descendants of Abraham to dwell in this land (Gen 12:1–3). This covenant was later confirmed to Abraham to be unconditional and everlasting (Gen 17:7, 8). Subsequently, the covenant was confirmed to his son Isaac in Gen 17:19, and then to his grandson Jacob in Gen 35:9–15.

God chose the children of Isaac, Abraham's son, to be

1. a witness to the true God of the universe before the nations;
2. a conduit to receive, preserve, and transmit Holy Scripture; and
3. the posterity for the messiah, the savior of the world.

GOD CHOSE *ERETZ YISRAEL* (THE LAND OF ISRAEL) TO BE THE CENTER OF THE WORLD

Israel has been on the crossroads of the great empires: Assyria, Babylonia, Egypt, Greece, and Rome. Israel has been "God's testing ground of faith." Israel has been, and still is, the place where God shows forth his miraculous power to sustain and bless his ancient people. God's covenant regarding the land is everlasting and unconditional.

God said to Abram, "For all the land which you see I give to you and your descendants forever. . . . Arise, walk in the land through its length and its width, for I give it to you" (Gen 13:15–17).

GOD CHOSE GENTILES TO HELP

> For the LORD will have mercy on Jacob, and will still choose Israel, and settle them in their own land. The strangers [Gentiles] will be joined with them. . . . People [Gentiles] will take them and bring them to their place. (Isa 14:1–2)

Behold, I will lift My hand in an oath to the nations [Gentiles], and set my banner for the peoples: They shall bring your sons in their arms, and your daughters shall be carried on their shoulders. (Isa 49:22)

GOD CHOSE PRECIOUS PROMISES

I will make you a great nation; I will bless you and make your name great and you shall be a blessing. I will bless those who bless you, and I will curse him who curses you; and in you all the families of the earth shall be blessed. (Gen 12:1–3)

DAY 12

Hallel: Psalms 113–118

Psalms 113–118 are read during Passover, Shavuot (Pentecost), Sukkot (Tabernacles), and Hanukkah to praise God for his power of redemption (salvation) and miraculous provision. They are not read during Rosh Hashanah or Yom Kippur—to read these jubilant psalms would not compatible with the somber nuance of the High Holy Days. These psalms are called the *Hallel*, which means "praise."

The hymns that were sung during the Lord's Passover meal (the Last Supper) were probably from the Hallel: Psalms 113–118.

PSALM 113

Praises God for being the great almighty who cares for even the least of us. He who is all-knowing, all-powerful, and everywhere present loves us.

PSALM 114

David reflects upon the sovereignty of God in freeing the Jews from bondage in the most powerful nation on earth and the miraculous survival in the wilderness, from the parting of the Sea to providing bread from heaven and water from the rock.

HALLEL: PSALMS 113-118

PSALM 115

Praises God for his salvation that only comes from Him. The psalm ends by saying "Hallelu-Yah"—praise the Lord.

PSALM 116

Praises God that he is able to rescue us from the worst possible danger that paralyzes our mind and spirit. And even if we die, we praise the Lord.

PSALM 117

The shortest psalm invites the nations to join the songs of thanksgiving and redemption. "Salvation is from the Jews," said Jesus to the woman (John 4:22). Israel is God's messenger to the world that he exists, and that his Yeshua (Jesus, "salvation") is for all the nations (Gen 12:1-3; Isa 43:10; Gal 3:29).

PSALM 118

David is thanking and praising God on behalf of Israel that deliverance has come. He saved his people from disaster and from death because of his unwavering love.

> From my distress I called upon the LORD: The LORD answered me. (Ps 118:5)

> It is better to take refuge in the LORD than to trust princes. (Ps 118:9)

> Give thanks to the LORD, for He is good: for His lovingkindness is everlasting. (Ps 118:29)

Time is short, life is precious, and Jesus is coming soon!

DAY 13

The Heart of Worship During Challenging Times!

When facing tragedy, we must prioritize our concentration! Our witness as believers becomes lackluster when we become preoccupied with self.

When captivated with God, we find that looking at ourselves diminishes in the shadow of his glory. The preoccupation with self fades immeasurably in the presence of the holy.

We become unaware of any goodness within ourselves or any "self"-esteem. Rather, we come to realize that we are deserving of death and hell, and that our only hope is found in the blood of the lamb.

Our focus must always become centered upon God and God alone. Any goodness or righteousness we may have comes from Messiah himself. In other words, Messiah's righteousness is "imputed" (credited) to those who are his sheep, to those who believe (2 Cor 5:21).

In the context of worship, as seen in many churches, the emphasis has changed to focus on self: "*It's all about me.*" Or, "It's about the band playing on stage, or the programs of feeling good about myself."

Authentic worship has always been about God, about his messiah, about seeking his face, and was never about the worshiper, or how the worshiper "feels."

The celebrant hovers between knowing that they are clean through the blood of the lamb and humbled by understanding that they deserve only banishment from a holy God.

> Who may ascend into the hill of the Lord? Or who may stand in His holy place? He who has clean hands and a pure heart. (Ps 24:3, 4)

When raising hands before God, one is saying with humility and reverence, *"Lord, look at my hands and see if there is any flaw, or sin, or anything that is not pleasing to you. I open my heart, my whole being, my soul, my life, and my actions before you. Is my worship acceptable to you?"*

A pure heart refers to our will being submissive to God's will in all matters. It involves humility and a right attitude before God. Going to the house of the Lord is a balance between "I was glad when they said to me, 'Let us go into the house of the Lord'" (Ps 122:1) and "Woe is me" (Isa 6:5)!

May we come back, as the song says, to "Be thou my vision, O Lord of my heart."

When our focus is redirected, we may find ourselves in a compelling position to effectively be "salt and light" in a very dark and frightening world.

DAY 14

Jerusalem

If I forget you, O Jerusalem,
Let my right hand forget its skill!—Ps 137:5

MARVEL AND MYSTERY

I marvel at the historic biblical mountains with their majestic peaks, trees, and stories. The Mount of Olives from the Temple Mount is glorious. The white sepulchers of the religious Jews who wish to be resurrected first when the messiah descends on the mount (Zech 14) are amassed on the slope of Olives. The steeple of the Church of Ascension atop the mount reminds us of Messiah's ascension to the Father. On the western face of the mountain, I behold the garden of Gethsemane and the place where Jesus rode triumphantly into Jerusalem. Jerusalem is filled with the mystery and wonder of the story of Messiah Jesus.

EMOTIONS ENGAGED

I experience the places where Jesus walked. The pool of Siloam. The pool of Bethesda, where Jesus healed a man. My heart is moved by the place where he stood before Pilate. I can touch the empty tomb and gaze upon Calvary. Oh, the religious experience is profound. Every emotion is engaged. I can be overwhelmed with all this information caressing my senses. I tremble and rejoice all at the same time. David walked this area, the prophets came here, and the apostles dwelt here.

COMMON COURAGE

And yet, everyday common people live here. They work long hours to scratch out a living. Everything is difficult here. Nothing is easy. I admire their strength, courage, and tenacity. Many Jews make their *aliyah* (moving to Israel) from other countries not knowing why they come. They just felt they had to relocate. Some come for religious reasons. Christians are here—very few, however. Jews and Muslims make up most of the population of Israel.

RULING AND REIGNING

Jerusalem has a powerful effect on people. After all, as the rabbis say, it is the "center of the earth." In fact, they emphasize it is the "center of the universe." In this, they are correct. Jerusalem is where Jesus will rule and reign for a thousand years. He will return to the Mount of Olives and then enter the city. No wonder Jerusalem creates fear and wonder in the hearts of men (Ps 48).[1]

The world hates the Jews being here in Israel. Yet God promised to bring them back from the four corners of the world (Isa 11:1, 12; 43:5–11; Jer 32:37; Ezek 37:21,22; Amos 9:13–15).

It is here, in Jerusalem and throughout Israel, that Israel Today Ministries provides meals and presents the gospel. Your financial partnership results in tens of thousands of meals provided for children, Holocaust survivors, and families.

Now in this world of fear and uncertainty, more than ever, we need your help to continue to be effective. Will you join us in

1. Johnson, *Divine Mysteries*, 184.

blessing God's ancient people? Will you consider a special gift to Israel Today Ministries? It's profoundly simple. "You give so they can live." Thank you for your generosity!

DAY 15

Here I Am!

HINENI—"HERE I AM"

Two of the greatest figures in the Bible are Abraham and Moses. Both were called by God. Both answered with the same Hebrew word, *Hineni* (He-nay-nee), "Here I am."

The word *Hineni* involves a willingness, a readiness, a conviction, no matter one's state of mind.

ABRAHAM

For Abraham (Gen 22), we read, "Then on the third day Abraham lifted his eyes and saw the place afar off" (v. 4). What place? The mountain where his son was to be killed, offered as a burnt offering to the Lord.

We do not know Abraham's state of mind. Some say he obeyed Elohim with absolute certainty. Others say he struggled through the night, rehearsing what God asked him to do. What would you feel? What would your state of mind be?

The word "Elohim," "God" (sovereign judge, the creator, architect of the universe), is used in verses 1, 3, 8, and 9 of Gen 22 until we arrive at the very moment of the greatest intensity in verse

11: "But, the angel of the LORD called to him from heaven and said, 'Abraham, Abraham!' So he said, 'Here I am.'"

There is a word change in the text. Now God is referred to as "YHVH" ("Adonai," or "HaShem") with uppercase letters ("LORD"), meaning "the unspeakable name of God," "the Name," or "the Merciful God," connected with love and mercy.

When the Lord called to Abraham in verse 11, he answered "*Hineni*"—"Here I am"—the same word used in verse 1. After the long, taxing journey, perhaps Abraham is now emotionally, as well as physically, exhausted; nevertheless, we find that Abraham still has a soul-deep conviction, a readiness to obey.

Again, "Elohim" is used in verse 12. However, in verse 14, Abraham worships and praises, stating that he "called the name of the place, The-LORD-Will-Provide; as it is said to this day, 'In the Mount of the LORD it shall be provided.'" In other words, the merciful unspeakable Name will provide. In the mountain of the merciful unspeakable Name, it will be seen; it will be provided.

MOSES

Similarly, when Moses came to the mountain of God (Elohim), the angel of the Lord (YHVH) appeared to him. When Moses looked a second time (turned aside to see), the Lord (YHVH) saw him. God (Elohim) called to him, and Moses answered, "*Hineni*" ("Here am I") (Exod 3:1–4).

God said, "I am the God (Elohim) of your father(s) Abraham, Isaac, and Jacob" (Exod 3:6). Then Moses was afraid to look upon Elohim. Then the Lord (YHVH) said, "I have seen the affliction of my people who are in Egypt. From this point forward we have the greatest story of national redemption told: the Passover" (a presage of Messiah our Passover; Exod 3:7).

In these stories, we see the merciful architect involved in human events. When he calls, we can choose to reject or accept. Rejecting his call can be easier. In accepting his call, difficulty may abound. However, when we are willing with unselfish conviction to hear God and then to follow God, no matter our circumstances or feelings, we will "see" God provide and move the universe according to our calling for his glory.

DAY 16

Puff of Air

Hebrew is a woven tapestry of profound and mysterious words that connect one Scripture verse to another.

The same Hebrew word used for Abel (*hevel*) is the same word used in Ecclesiastes translated "vanity" (Hebrew *hevel*, meaning "fleeting breath" or "puff of air").

"'Vanity of vanities,' says the Preacher; 'vanity of vanities, all is vanity'" (Eccl 1:2). As Abel's life was just a moment, a puff of air, a fleeting breath, so is our life. Scripture reminds us of our temporary time on earth, and that is not a bad thing.

We all have hopes and dreams, but many do not come to fruition. We all accomplish moments of magnificence with grand applause, and then they are soon forgotten, and the applause is silenced. We all desperately attempt to stop the aging process only to find limitations in our struggle as we become weakened over time.

Again, it is not a bad thing to be reminded that our time on earth is short and to understand that our breath is momentary and that our seven, eight, or nine decades of life eventually come to an end. Realizing these truths, we should find ourselves reevaluating our lives and asking, "*What do I want my last footprint to be?*"

We are never too old or too young to ask such an important question. Recalibrate what's important, then start making the necessary changes and walk toward the goal of making your life count for Jesus, your family, neighbors, and of course Israel.

The sensory word *hevel* ("fleeting breath" or "puff of air") makes us all reconsider our priorities. A reality check indeed. However, it is necessary if we are to grow in our spiritual walk, making an effective difference by being "light" in this dark world, building the kingdom of God.

DAY 17

Waiting!

If there is one thing our culture hates, it's waiting. We want a quick fix to our problems, and we want to have things now. We want the title, degree, position, and accolades without the hard work involved to achieve such things—so we look for shortcuts. If our iPhone loses the Wi-Fi connection or the stoplight seems long, we become frustrated, even angry. We think we are wasting time when we wait for something.

HOPE

In Scripture, waiting relates to hope—not wasting time. The Hebrew word for "hope" is *tikvah*, like that of the Israeli national athem, Hatikvah, and is from the root *qavah* which means "wait."

Hoping for something is intimately related to waiting for that something to happen. "My soul, wait silently for God alone, For my expectation [hope, *tikvah*] is from Him" (Ps 62:5). "I wait [*qavah*] for the Lord, my soul waits [*qavah*]" (Ps 130:5).

CORD

Rahab let down the scarlet line, or cord, to protect her home from the coming invasion. The Hebrew word translated "line" or "cord" is *tikvah* or "hope" (Josh 2:18). Rahab had found hope and waited for redemption and rescue.

SLOTHA

Jesus spoke Aramaic, Hebrew, and probably Greek. The disciple said to Jesus, "Teach us to pray" (Luke 11:1). The Aramaic word for prayer is *slotha*. It means to set a trap, to wait—emphasizing the patience and silence of a hunter, waiting, listening for the crackling of the leaves or grass, thus finding the reward of your perseverance. It is not wasting time. The answer will come. You must be patient; you must be silent; you must wait; you must have hope. Waiting seems to be the rule; it can be a difficult thing to do, waiting, waiting . . . to hope for something.

Waiting is hoping. Hoping is like a cord fastened to something very strong. To what, or to whom, is our cord fastened? For the believer, it should be God. "For You are my hope [*tikvah*], O Lord God" (Ps 71:5).

THE RULE

Both Sarah and Hannah waited and waited to have a child. The Jewish refugees in Babylon waited seventy years to be released and the Jewish slaves in Egypt waited for four hundred years for their freedom. The 120 disciples of Jesus waited in the upper room for a promise to be fulfilled. Peter being in jail waited for liberation.

The children were eventually born. Freedom from the seventy years in Babylon came as Cyrus released the refugees, and the miracle of Passover happened after four hundred years of slavery in Egypt. The promise of the Holy Spirit eventually was manifested upon the disciples empowering the church, and Peter was miraculously liberated from prison.

Waiting is the rule. Our hope comes to fruition in time—not our time, but in God's time. We wait for it. "But if we hope for what we do not see, we eagerly wait for it with perseverance" (Rom 8:25).

DAY 18

Waking Up!

Waking up in the morning can be overwhelming for some people. Facing the stress and anxiety of daily tasks such as paying bills, answering emails, scheduling children's activities, managing one's health, and the negative world news can be devastating to emotional health. No wonder people are depressed, tired, and perhaps sickly.

There is a prayer that Jews have prayed for thousands of years every morning:

> Hear, O Israel: The LORD our God, the LORD *is* one! You shall love the LORD your God with all your heart, with all your soul, and with all your strength. And these words which I command you today shall be in your heart. You shall teach them diligently to your children, and shall talk of them when you sit in your house, when you walk by the way, when you lie down, and when you rise up. You shall bind them as a sign on your hand, and they shall be as frontlets between your eyes. You shall write them on the doorposts of your house and on your gates. —Deut 6: 4–9

This prayer is called the *Shema*, which means "hear or listen." This prayer directs us to action. It focuses our attention upon God first thing in the morning and not upon the world or the busyness of the day.

Jesus would say, "He who has ears, let him hear." He is saying, "Hear the words and obey"—put it into action. Every morning Jesus and his disciples would pray this prayer. To meditate upon and pray these words first thing in the morning will recalibrate your mind, attitude, and direction as you address your busy day.

As you reflect upon God through this prayer, remember one of the names of God is El Shaddai, which is often translated "God Almighty." The name also implies another trait of God, that of sufficiency. The Hebrew word *shad* from *Shad-dai* means "chest" or "bosom"—a breast. Whenever a Hebrew word ends with *ai*, it usually means a plurality, a pair, and at times personal possession: "my"; "God is my sufficiency."

A breast symbolizes nurturing, maternal love, and sustenance. In other words, the name El Shaddai not only means "God who is almighty," but it also means "God who is all-sufficient."

As you start your day in prayer, be reminded that God is "all -sufficient" and can meet your every need for the day—however overwhelming things seem to be. He's got you (Isa 41:13).

May El Shaddai bless you beyond measure as you seek him!

DAY 19

A Mother's Plea!

2 KINGS 4:2-7

Sometimes we feel like there is no hope. The doctor gave us a bad report, or a financial need is greater than we realized.

Despair at times seems to overwhelm us. Nothing short of a miracle will help.

Sometimes our feeling of being overwhelmed can blind us from seeing what is right in front of us.

Scripture tells us that the universe is governed by established laws. However, God (or God's messengers) can perform acts we call *miracles* that defy such laws.

There is a story in the Bible that describes the wife of Obadiah, who found herself deeply in debt after her husband's death (2 Kgs 4).

Her husband was a student of the prophets, perhaps preparing for the ministry, and he loved the Lord passionately.

He died apparently prematurely, and the creditors were knocking on her door threatening to take her two boys as slaves to pay off the debt. (This was common practice in that day.)

She pleaded with Elisha to help her. Elisha asked, "What do you have in the house?" She replied, "Nothing in the house but a jar of oil." (I assume this was olive oil as it is plentiful in that part of the world.)

The prophet told her to go to her neighbors and ask for a lot of empty jars. Then he said to go inside her house and begin to fill the jars with her oil.

She filled each jar to the brim. She asked for another jar, but there were no jars left.

She had filled each of the jars she had gathered, and then she sold the oil, paid off her debt, and had enough left over for her and her two sons.

No one knows how much oil she originally had. Some say little, and some say so minute as to only smear a bit on the little finger. Whatever the amount, a miracle took place.

If the prophet alone had the power to perform the miracle, why did he ask the woman, "What do you have in the house"?

Good question! Was it necessary for her to have a small amount of oil for the miracle to occur? Yes.

There had to be a starting point for the miracle to take place.

Jesus would do a similar thing in John 2 when he turned six jars of water into wine. There had to be something tangible to be the point of reference for the miracle.

God has given each of us a little oil or empty jars or something that he can use and miraculously transform from paucity to plenty.

Sometimes we feel like there is no hope. Sometimes our feeling of being overwhelmed can blind us from seeing what is right in front of us.

Emulate Obadiah's wife by moving forward and start to pour, using what God has given you, while believing that something will happen.

DAY 20

A Mother's Concern!

JOHN 2:1-10

John is the most mystical of the Gospel writers. Each word, each nuance, has a greater meaning.

In John chapter 2, we find Jesus's first miracle. Notice how John begins:

VERSE 1: "On the third day there was a wedding in Cana of Galilee."

There were four days numbered in the first chapter. Here he states "on the third day." The wedding occurred on Tuesday, or the third day of week. The third day of a week in the Torah is very important. In Gen 1:9-13 the phrase "God saw that it was good" is stated twice (vv. 10, 12). The wedding happened on the third day of the week, evoking, in the Jewish mind, the idea of God's double blessing upon the event. Today, many Jewish weddings happen on Tuesday.

The four days enumerated by John in the first chapter, plus the third day, is a seven-day sequence from 1:19—2:11 which alludes to the seven days in the first chapter of Genesis having to do with God's creative power.

John is trying to tell us something wonderful here.

A MOTHER'S CONCERN!

There was also a similar revelation on the morning of the third day when Moses went up the mountain to receive the Torah, the revelation of God:

> Then it came to pass on the third day, in the morning, that there were thunderings and lightnings, and a thick cloud on the mountain; and the sound of the trumpet was very loud, so that all the people who were in the camp trembled. (Exod 19:16)
>
> Surely the LORD our God has shown us His glory and His greatness, and we have heard His voice. (Deut 5:24)

VERSE 3: "The mother of Jesus said to Him, 'They have no wine.'"

The symbols of a wedding on the third day and wine were important symbols of God's blessing.

To run out of wine would have been terrible, the ultimate insult to the guests and host.

VERSE 6: "There were set there six waterpots of stone, according to the manner of purification of the Jews, containing twenty or thirty gallons apiece."

Each guest was expected to wash their hands. Washing their hands was a symbol of washing away "spiritual uncleanness"—impurities. Therefore, the water was dirty, murky, impure, unclean.

VERSE 7: "Jesus said to them, 'Fill the waterpots with water.' And they filled them up to the brim."

The six stone waterpots, containing twenty to thirty gallons each, would have been around 150 gallons with servings of one cup each, which could accommodate 2400 servings—overflowing.

VERSES 8-10: We find they drew the water out and took it to the master of the feast, who took it to the bridegroom, and all were amazed at the quality—the best wine ever tasted.

What is John telling us? The seven-day sequence and the third-day emphasis lead us to understand that the miracle of dirty water turned into the best wine is a miracle of creation—a revelation that "all things were made through Him, and without Him nothing was made that was made" (John 1:3).

He took that which was impure and made it pure. Jesus is Lord of creation, Lord over time. "Before Abraham was, I AM," said Jesus (John 8:58), emphasizing that he is before time and he is after time—he eternally is.

Wine needs time to age; it took only a split second to turn murky water into the choicest wine. Jesus had come to bring about conversion: water to wine, sinners to saints.

John sees in the wedding miracle a beginning of God's revelation of salvation found in the incarnated God-man, Messiah Jesus. Using the juxtaposition between creation (Gen 1) hinting at the revelation on Sinai (Exod 19) and focusing our attention that Jesus is God in the flesh dwelling among us (John 1:14) and "a light to *bring* revelation to the Gentiles, and the glory of Your people Israel" (Luke 2:32), we arrive at the conclusion that "where sin abounded, grace abounded much more" (Rom 5:20).

After the resurrection, the apostles were anticipating the Lord's return. Recalling the wedding in Cana, they were reminded that John 2 also alludes to the overflowing wine in the latter years when Jews began to return to Israel:

> "Behold, the days are coming," says the LORD, "When . . . the mountains shall drip with sweet wine, and all the hills shall flow *with it*" (Amos 9:13).

> [Jesus said,] "For I say to you, you shall see Me no more till you say, 'Blessed *is* He who comes in the name of the LORD!'" (Matt 23:29)

And indeed, by the thousands, Jews are coming to faith in Messiah Yeshua. The mountains are beginning to "drip with sweet wine."

DAY 21

Image of God!

So God created man in His own image; in the image of God created He him; male and female He created them. —Gen 1:27

Moses tells us that human beings are a special part of God's creation.

God created us in his own image, "in the image of God (*tzelem Elohim*)." The Hebrew word for "image" is *tzelem* and connects to another Hebrew word: *tzel*, meaning "shadow."

A shadow appears when light falls upon us. According to Holy Scripture, humans are created in God's image, a shadow or figure of God. God's presence and light (Shekinah) overshadowed Adam as he "kissed" (or breathed into) his nostrils. As God breathed the breath of life into Adam, his divine presence did cast a shadow.

Human beings (though flawed by sin) reflect or shadow God's beauty and holiness. To illumine the shadow, a human being will only find completeness and peace by trusting and putting their eternal future in Messiah Jesus.

Another word joins with the Hebrew word for "image": Bezalel, which was the name of the person chosen by God to create the tabernacle (Exod 31). Bezalel means "in the shadow of God." The tabernacle made it possible for anyone to come near to God; it provided a very special connection to the divine.

When we come near to God and worship him, we are in his very presence, in his shadow, and under his wings, which is a reference to the Shekinah, the divine presence of God (Ps 91:1–4).

POINTS TO PONDER

1. Believers rest in his shadow, under his wings, caused by the light of his glory (Shekinah), for God protects them (Ps 91:1, 4).
2. Believers are secure in the "shadow," caused by the light/glory (Shekinah) of the Almighty, and are protected as God will never abandon his children.
3. Believers have peace and assurance that God can be known and is known.
4. Believers have been accepted in the beloved (Eph 1:5–7).

These truths are humbling. We do not deserve God's mercy—he doesn't owe us anything.

Nevertheless, through his love, mercy, and grace, God makes it possible for anyone to come near to him in a personal relationship through the blood of Messiah Jesus: "To the praise of the glory of His grace, by which He made us accepted in the Beloved. In Him we have redemption through His blood, the forgiveness of sins, according to the riches of His grace" (Eph 1:6–7).

DAY 22

Ancient Words

The words that I speak to you are spirit, and they are *life.*
—John 6:63

It is important to remember good words. Below are ancient words to remember with all our strength, mind, and heart:

WORDS TO REMEMBER

Pray

>Pray for the peace of Jerusalem: "May they prosper who love you." (Ps 122:6)

Do

>Inasmuch as you did *it* to one of the least of these My brethren, you did *it* to Me. (Matt 25:40)

Bless

> For he who touches you [Israel] touches the apple of His eye. (Zech 2:8)

Benefits

> Now the LORD had said to Abram . . . "I will bless those who bless you, And I will curse him who curses you." (Gen 12:1, 3)

A Chosen People

> For you *are* a holy people to the LORD your God; the LORD your God has chosen you to be a people for Himself, a special treasure above all the peoples on the face of the earth. (Deut 7:6)

> "You *are* My witnesses," says the LORD,
> "And My servant whom I have chosen,
> That you may know and believe Me,
> And understand that I *am* He.
> Before Me there was no God formed,
> Nor shall there be after Me.
> I, *even* I, *am* the LORD,
> And besides Me *there is* no savior."
> (Isa 43:10–11)

A Chosen Land

> Thus says the LORD GOD: "This is Jerusalem; I have set her in the midst of the nations and the countries all around her." (Ezek 5:5)

Belongs to God

> For the land *is* Mine; for you *are* strangers and sojourners with Me. (Lev 25:23)

To Abraham's Seed

> And I will establish My covenant between Me and you and your descendants after you in their generations, for an everlasting covenant, to be God to you and your descendants after you. Also I give to you and your descendants after you the land in which you are a stranger, all the land of Canaan, as an everlasting possession; and I will be their God. (Gen 17:7–8)

Given to Isaac

> And Abraham said to God, "Oh, that Ishmael might live before You!" Then God said: "No, Sarah your wife shall bear you a son, and you shall call his name Isaac; I will establish My covenant with him for an everlasting covenant, *and* with his descendants after him." (Gen 17:18–19)

Our Centerpiece

> Hear, O Israel: The LORD our God, the LORD *is* one! You shall love the LORD your God with all your heart, with all your soul, and with all your strength. (Deut 6:4–5)

Our Children

And these words which I command you today shall be in your heart. You shall teach them diligently to your children, and shall talk of them when you sit in your house, when you walk by the way, when you lie down, and when you rise up. (Deut 6:6–7)

Our Assignment

Walk about Zion, And go all around her. Count her towers;
Mark well her bulwarks; Consider her palaces;
That you may tell *it* to the generation following. (Ps 48:12–13)

Our Life

Jesus said to him, "I am the way, the truth, and the life. No one comes to the Father except through Me." (John 14:6)

Our Mission

And Jesus came and spoke to them, saying, "All authority has been given to Me in heaven and on earth. Go therefore and make disciples of all the nations, baptizing them in the name of the Father and of the Son and of the Holy Spirit, teaching them to observe all things that I have commanded you; and lo, I am with you always, *even* to the end of the age." Amen. (Matt 28:18–20)

DAY 23

Long Nose!

MOSES

When Moses came down the mountain (Exod 32), he found the Israelites worshiping a golden calf. In his anger, he cast the tablets which he received from God and broke them at the foot of the holy mountain.

After meting out a swift and severe punishment upon those who sinned against God, in which three thousand people fell that day, Moses meets with God once again (Exod 33).

FACE TO FACE

In verse 11 of Exod 33, it is said that "the LORD spoke with Moses face to face" (Hebrew *p'anim al p'anim*). Face to face is a very intimate position. *P'anim* not only means "face," but "interior," or "inside." A face exposes a person. Unless you are a good actor, your face reveals the intimate character of your heart.

KISSING

When one kisses, it is face to face, and very intimate. The Shulamite stated, "Let him kiss me with the kisses of his mouth" (Song 1:2). She was desirous for Solomon to be close and personal.

BREATHING

As God "breathed" into his "nostrils," Adam became a living being ("breathed," Hebrew *naphach*: to blow, puff, inflate; "nostrils," Hebrew root *apf [af]*, nose; "living being," Hebrew *nephesh chayee*, "living soul"). This early episode was a very intimate face-to-face moment between the Creator and the creature (Gen 2:7).

ESSENCE

Similarly, when God spoke to Moses "face to face," it was very intimate—an otherworldly moment. Moses asked the Lord, "Please, show me your glory!" God replied, "You cannot see my face, for mankind shall not see me and live!" Then the Lord said, "Behold, there is a place by me, and you shall stand there on the rock; and it will come about, while my glory is passing by, that I will put you in the cleft of the rock and cover you with my hand until I have passed by. Then I will take my hand away and you shall see my back, but my face shall not be seen" (Exod 33:18–23).

God was about to reveal something about his character—a manifestation and glimpse of his essence. We easily see the evidence of his work or his "energy" in the creation of the stars, planets, all material life and substance. However, only in part do we understand his essence, his otherness. He is about to divulge something profound to the prophet.

LONG NOSE

> And the LORD passed before him and proclaimed, "The LORD, the LORD God, merciful and gracious, longsuffering." (Exod 34:6)

Here we find God's response to a rebellious people. However, I want to focus upon the word translated "longsuffering," or "slow to anger." In Hebrew it is two words, *arek aph*, which literally means "long nose." *Aph*, or nose/nostrils, is associated with the face. When a person is angry, his nostrils flare, and you know he is angry. His face shows what he is feeling on the inside. God is saying to Moses, "I have a 'long nose.'" In other words, "It takes me a very long time to flare my nostrils." Thus, I am "slow to anger," or "longsuffering."

Once this mysterious revelation of God's essence was made clear to Moses, he "bowed his head toward the earth, and worshiped" (Exod 34:8).

God is a merciful God, slow to anger, slow to wrath: "Father, forgive them, for they do not know what they do" (Luke 23:34).

IT DOESN'T MATTER

Beloved, it doesn't matter have far off course we have gone, nor what we have done or haven't done. God has a "long nose" and is slow to anger. He is longsuffering, and like the father of the son gone astray, as you return to him, God will see you from afar and will have compassion on you and fall on you and kiss your face (Luke 15:20).

Trust him, for "The LORD, the LORD God, [is] merciful and gracious, longsuffering."

DAY 24

Deep Waters

*And Moses said to the people, "Do not be afraid. Stand still, and see the salvation [Yeshua, Jesus] of the L*ORD*, which He will accomplish for you today. For the Egyptians whom you see today, you shall see again no more forever. The L*ORD *will fight for you, and you shall hold your peace [keep silent]." And the L*ORD *said to Moses, "Why do you cry to Me? Tell the children of Israel to go forward."*—Exod 14:13–15

Bodies of water have caused problems for God's people in the Bible: the flood of Noah, the Red Sea for Moses, the Jordan River holding back Israel from crossing into the promised land, and the stormy Sea of Galilee that caused great fear for the disciples.

When believers face deep waters, God shows up (in fact, he is always present) and provides a way forward. Noah's family was saved, the Israelites crossed the Red Sea and the Jordan River safely, and Jesus calmed the storm.

Whatever situation in which you may find yourself, whether stress, fear, or uncertainty, God will provide and give you strength to move forward.

Just as the Spirit of God was hovering over the troubled waters of creation and brought order into the universe, so it will be with you. He will provide a way and an answer.

Our part? "Go forward!" No retreat. No quitting.

Whatever is blocking or standing in your way, God says, "Do not be afraid. See the salvation (Yeshua, Jesus) of the Lord. The Lord will fight for you, and you shall hold your peace (keep silent)." *Go forward.*

DAY 25

Jesus Received Worship

Who does that? Who receives worship? Jesus told Satan, "Away with you, Satan! For it is written, 'You shall worship the Lord your God, and Him only you shall serve'" (Matt 4:10).

Jesus was saying to Satan, "Don't test me, asking me to worship you. You must worship God only!"

HOW THEN, DID JESUS RECEIVE WORSHIP?

In the past:

1. The magi worshiped Jesus when he was a child: "And when they had come into the house, they saw the young Child with Mary His mother, and fell down and worshiped Him" (Matt 2:11).

2. The man born blind worshiped him: "Then he said, 'Lord, I believe!' And he worshiped Him"(John 9:38).

3. The frightened disciples worshiped him: "Then those who were in the boat came and worshiped Him, saying, 'Truly You are the Son of God'" (Matt 14:33).

4. The women worshiped him: "So they came and held Him by the feet and worshiped Him" (Matt 28:9).

5. The startled disciples worshiped him and found great joy: "And they worshiped Him, and returned to Jerusalem with great joy" (Luke 24:52).

In the future:

1. Everyone will worship him: "That at the name of Jesus every knee should bow, of those in heaven, and of those on earth, and of those under the earth" (Phil 2:10).

2. The elders will worship him: "And the twenty-four elders fell down and worshiped Him who lives forever and ever" (Rev 5:14).

Jesus never rebuked anyone for worshiping him. He corrected those who scolded others for worshiping him when Martha was upset that Mary sat at his feet and when the disciples were indignant when a woman anointed him (Luke 10:42; Matt 26:10).

Men may receive temporary accolades and kudos, but only God is worshiped.

Jesus was/is worshiped.

Jesus is God: "I and My Father are one" (John 10:30).

Worship him and rejoice!

DAY 26

Love First Mentioned!

The word "love" (Hebrew, *ahav*) is first mentioned in Gen 22:2: "Then He said, 'Take now your son, your only *son* Isaac, whom you love, and go to the land of Moriah, and offer him there as a burnt offering on one of the mountains of which I shall tell you.'"

Abraham is reminded of his most cherished possession of his life. "Only" son (Hebrew *yachid*, "the unique one," "one and only") has the same idea as "only begotten." Isaac was the "promised (one)," the child that was foretold.

There is a soberness, a holiness, to this moment. We can hear the echo of what God said to Moses: "Take your sandals off your feet, for the place where you stand is holy ground" (Exod 3:5).

"WHOM YOU LOVE" (HEBREW *ASHER AHAVTA*)

As far as the record goes, Abraham believed God and was willing to make the supreme sacrifice: to take his son and to slay him upon the altar in order that he might please him who called him from darkness into light. This reminds us most vividly of John 3:16: "For God so loved the world that He gave His only begotten Son."

Moriah (eight centuries later) became the site of the temple where all the sacrifices were offered, where God ripped the veil in two so that free access to the holy of holies might be made for all the people of God. This is the same mountain in which Jesus was crucified for our sins.

SLEEPLESS NIGHT

It is written that Abraham got up "early" in the morning (Gen 22:3). I don't believe Abraham slept that night. Perhaps he wrestled and agonized with God as he did for Sodom and Gomorrah, even with greater pathos.

I find an interesting parallel in the fact that Jesus, "early" in the morning of his crucifixion after the evening of the Passover Seder, came to Gethsemane.

The Scriptures tell us that he "began to be troubled and deeply distressed" (Mark 14:33). There he agonized, wrestling with his Father, praying, "Father, if it is Your will, take this cup away from Me; nevertheless not My will, but Yours, be done" (Luke 22:42).

It is fitting that the Lord went to Gethsemane. Gethsemane means "wine press" or "oil press." That fateful morning of betrayal and arrest, the record tells us that "being in agony, He [Jesus] prayed more earnestly. Then His sweat became like great drops of blood falling down to the ground" (Luke 22:44). He was being "pressed," yielding to his Father's will and purpose.

And so it was with Abraham that dreadful night.

> Then on the third day Abraham lifted [raised] his eyes and saw. (Gen 22:4)

For those three days, in Abraham's mind, Isaac was dead. And yet, on this day, the third day, Abraham declared, "The lad and I will go yonder and worship, and we will come back to you" (Gen 22:5). (Jesus was dead for three days, and rose on the third day.)

He believed, somehow, that they would "come back." By faith Abraham, when he was tested, offered up Isaac, concluding that God was able to raise him up, even from the dead (Heb 11:17–19).

Isaac, who was around thirty years old, willingly submitted to this "binding" upon the altar. This episode is called the *Akedah* in Hebrew, which means "the binding."

The second time the word "love" is found in Scripture is Gen 24:67: "And he loved her [*va-yeehaveha*]. So Isaac was comforted."

Could it be that Isaac learned how to love Rebekah sacrificially with every part of his being by remembering his father's love on that day long ago?

God provided the ram for Abraham (Gen 22:12, 13). This is a picture of Jesus becoming our substitute, paying the ultimate price for our sins.

The ram has played a significant role throughout biblical history. Its skin provided a mantle for Elijah. It was used to make the strings of David's harp. Its two horns represented the two trumpets, one to be sounded at the great revelation of God at Mount Sinai and the other to be blown at the coming of the messiah (the "last trump"; 1 Cor 15:52).

> And Abraham called the name of that place, The-LORD-Will-Provide [Jehovah-Jireh]; as it is said to this day, "In the Mount of the Lord it shall be provided [seen]." (Gen 22:14)

Jehovah-Jireh means "the Lord will provide" or "the Lord will see to it."

Isaac is a type of the Lord Jesus Christ up to a certain point, and then the ram takes his place and becomes God's provision for the sinner. Abraham understood all the meaning of these things. We hear Jesus saying in John 8:56, "Father Abraham rejoiced to see My day, and he saw *it* and was glad."

DAY 27

The Fifth Directive!

Biblical Judaism and Christian faith is built upon collective wisdom from the prophets, apostles, and sacred writings that were passed down from parent to child through the millennia.

Gentiles who believe in Messiah Jesus are grafted into the olive tree of faith in the God of Abraham, Isaac, and Jacob (Rom 11) and have become included—no longer excluded—from the commonwealth of Israel, thus becoming fellow citizens with the saints of God's household, Messiah Jesus himself being the cornerstone that holds it all together (Eph 2, 3).

As believers, we must pass down to our children and grandchildren this collective wisdom from the prophets and apostles.

Did you ever wonder why the fifth commandment to honor one's father and mother was at the bottom of the first tablet? Jewish sages emphasize that it is the foundation upon which our initial understanding of God rests. It is the father's and mother's duty and privilege to pass down this collective wisdom to their children, bringing them to the knowledge of a holy God.

Not only do we receive our very life, DNA, unique upbringing, gifts, challenges, and idiosyncracies from our parents; they also give us guidance, teaching us values and God's purpose for our life.

You may say, "My experience growing up was full of difficulty, not having godly parents." Remember David's words: "When my father and my mother forsake me, Then the Lord will take care of me. Teach me Your way, O Lord, And lead me in a smooth [right] path" (Ps 27:10–11). Ponder the truth that God thinks about you all the time and created you for this moment. You are no mistake—God makes no mistakes (Ps 139)!

If you are a parent, or someday will become a parent, be challenged by the fifth commandment, passing down to the next generation the collective wisdom that stems from the prophets, apostles, and sacred writings, focusing upon Messiah Jesus, the cornerstone, and in so doing, you will give your children a good reason to honor you.

DAY 28

You Will Know!

James the Just (Hebrew *Ya'akov Hatzaddik*), was Jesus's (Yeshua's) brother and chief rabbi/leader of Jerusalem's Messianic Jewish community found in the book of Acts. He said these words in Jas 2:18: "But someone will say, 'You have faith, and I have works.' Show me your faith without your works, and I will show you my faith by my works."

The bottom line of what he said is that a true faith, that which changes people, should be exhibited via good works. He emphasizes that it is impossible to express a faith without deeds/actions.

I teach my students in seminary, "You will know what I believe by what I do and where I go." Scripture has much to say about this, and Hebrew cultural nuance underscores that you are known by what you do, not so much as by what you say.

Words come easy. Actions are more difficult. Some actions are found in the distinct virtues, the fruit of the Spirit, as categorized by Paul (Gal 5:22-23). Jesus fed people, then taught them. This is the model of Israel Today Ministries. We bless people, meeting their needs, then we speak.

DAY 29

Women with "Fire"!

Paul was blessed to have godly women working with him in ministry. Here is a list for you to peruse: Chloe, Priscilla, Phoebe, Mary, Junia, Tryphaena, Tryphosa, Persis, the mother of Rufus, Julia, Olympas, Euodia, Syntyche, Nympha, Apphia, Claudia (1 Cor 1:11; 16:19; Rom 16:1, 3, 6, 7, 12, 13, 15; Phil 4:2; Col 4:15; Phlm 2; 2 Tim 4:19, 21, respectively).

Historically, women have been at the center of prayer groups, bible study groups, church logistics, and revivals. In fact, the very first words of man had to do with a woman, who changed everything.

FIRST WORDS OF MAN

> And Adam said: "This *is* now bone of my bones, and flesh of my flesh; She shall be called Woman, because she was taken out of Man." (Gen 2:23)

Adam found his proper mate in Eve, the first woman. Adam had given names to all the creatures and did not find one suitable for him—until Eve.

He said, "She shall be called Woman, because she was taken out of Man." The Hebrew word for man is *ish*, "eesh". The Hebrew word for woman is *isha*, "ee-shah." It is a Hebraic wordplay on the feminine form of the Hebrew word for man (*ish*).

Adam named all the creatures and had found none among them worthy or resembling of his name; however, Eve deserved to be given a name equivalent to his own.

The root which *isha* derives from is *ansh*, meaning "fragility" and "delicacy." The word "fire" (*ish*) resonates in this beautiful, complex, and interesting word for woman (*isha*). Therefore, the word "woman" means "fragile," "delicate," and "fire."

History holds witness to these noted qualities of a woman. Godly women are adorned with gentle and quiet spirits, which is precious in the sight of God (1 Pet 3:4, 5). But wait. There is that quality of "fire."

WOMEN WHO HAD "FIRE"

Scripture is replete with women of God who had gentle and quiet spirits, but they had "fire"—a courage beyond measure. Here are a few below.

Shiprah and Puah

Instead of killing the Hebrew children, as ordered by the king of Egypt, they saved them. These women had "fire" by fearing God and honoring him by saving human life at the risk of their own lives for disobeying the king (Exod 1:15–22).

Lois and Eunice

Lois was Timothy's grandma and Eunice was his mom. They both taught Timothy by word and deed how to live for and to follow God. They had a profound impact on Timothy at a young age. In turn, he influenced the spread of the gospel throughout the first century, facing persecution and hardships. Within a wicked pagan Roman Empire, these two women had "fire" and were steadfast in their faith, standing against the culture of evil teaching their son and grandson how to live for God (2 Tim 3:14, 15).

Abigail

Abigail was the wife of a wicked man, Nabal. He had turned down a request from David's men for provisions after they were kind to him. Abigail knew that David would respond in wrath. She took provisions to David and pleaded with him not to take revenge upon her husband and household. Abigail was courageous and took incredible risks by helping David as her husband could have punished her harshly for her actions, and/or David could have punished her by being associated with Nabal. Her "fire" led her to bless others and save her household, and eventually to become David's wife (1 Sam 25).

Deborah

Her story is told in both prose (Judg 4) and poetry (Judg 5). She was a judge, warrior, prophet, poet, songwriter, and singer. God told Deborah to go to Mount Tabor and attack Sisera, who was Jabin's commander of troops. She contacted Barak, a renowned Israeli warrior, and commanded him to bring ten thousand troops up to the mountain. Together they were victorious in battle against a superior army. Deborah was obedient to God, courageous, and had "fire" in her being. No matter how difficult the odds were, she stood true to God's word.

Women with "fire" shine throughout history!

DAY 30

Raising Hands!

Who may ascend into the hill of the LORD? Or who may stand in His holy place? He who has clean hands and a pure heart, Who has not lifted up his soul to an Idol, Nor sworn deceitfully. He shall receive blessing from the LORD, and righteousness from the God of his salvation. —Ps 24:3–5

Psalm 24 is a hymn of David celebrating God as the creator and conqueror. It is used in Jewish liturgy, an entrance liturgy (vv. 3–6; Ps 5; 15) on holy days when the Torah scroll is returned to the ark. The psalm has two parts divided by the "*Selah.*" Each part asks questions and then answers the questions. Perhaps this psalm was sung antiphonally.

VERSE 1: Here we find that HaShem (YHVH) owns the earth—it belongs to him. He chose a hill to be the place where his presence would be made known.

The hill? Mount Moriah. *Abraham* bound Isaac on Moriah; *David* bought the threshing floor on top of Moriah; *Solomon* built the Temple atop the threshing floor; *Jesus* was crucified, died, buried and rose again on Moriah (Gen 22; 1 Chr 21; 2 Chr 3; Gospels). The earth is his "footstool" and his presence was revealed in the holy of holies (Isa 66:1).

Verse 3: Since his presence, his glory, is revealed in the temple, "who may ascend... [and] stand in His holy place?" Good question!

It's an ethical and moral question. David asked this same question before in Ps 15:1, and the prophet Isaiah addresses the same in Isa 33:14, 15.

Before worshipers would ascend the holy hill, before they would approach the temple, they would go through the "mikvah," the Jewish ritual bath: self-immersion (baptism) at the foot of Mount Moriah or Mount Zion, which is next to Mount Moriah. It was an act of spiritual preparation and purification.

Verse 4: "He who has clean hands and a pure heart, who has not lifted up his soul to an idol, nor sworn deceitfully."

Before you "ascend," one must have clean hands. Raising hands is not an Evangelical or Pentecostal invention. Raising hands was an expression of worship thousands of years ago with Jewish believers. When worshipers raised their hands, it was an intimate, holy form of reverence.

One must have clean hands in terms of his dealings with others. One must be a person of integrity and honesty. One must have a reverence, a humble attitude before God. There is joy and fear in raising clean hands. The Holy Spirit generates the joy, and respect of the presence of a holy God generates the fear.

When raising hands before God, one is saying with humility and reverence, *"Lord, look at my hands and see if there is any flaw, or sin, or anything that is not pleasing to you. I open my heart, my whole being, my soul, my life, and my actions before you. Is my worship acceptable to you?"*

A "pure heart" refers to our will being submissive to God's will in all matters. It involves humility and a right attitude before God. Going to the house of the Lord is a balance between "I was glad when they said to me, 'Let us go into the house of the Lord'" (Ps 122:1) and "Woe is me!" (Isa 6:5).

"Who has not lifted up his soul" implies elevating one's life, self, person, and mind falsely, deceiving oneself with a life devoid of righteousness and good works. Simply, the one who has not lifted up his soul is the one who is lying before God, attempting to speak his name for personal gain through an act of false worship.

Idol or a Falsehood; Deceitfully: "To raise in vain" your hands. Raising your hand and voicing a false oath ("pledge" or "vow") or acting out an expression of holiness as though to an idol is a miserable and heartbreaking condition. Sadness eventually overwhelms the soul because of the hypocrisy. The one who seeks to grow spiritually must upgrade his behavior.

The one who seeks to grow spiritually must upgrade his behavior.

VERSE 5: "He shall receive blessing from the LORD, and righteousness from the God of his salvation."

Those who approach God purely, properly, and humbly shall receive and carry a blessing. He will lift up the blessing from God and praise him. It is a blessing that affects the rest of his life, producing righteousness he receives from God.

Because he honors God, God blesses him. God knows his behavior and heart, for his hands are clean: "Look at my hands and see!" God sees and rewards accordingly!

> Oh, worship the LORD in the beauty of holiness! Tremble before Him, all the earth. —Ps 96:9

DAY 31

Charity, Duty, Love!

Tzedakah, "seh-dah-kuh," is the Hebrew word for the acts we call "charity": giving aid, assistance, and money towards helping the poor and needy.

The word *tzedakah* is derived from the Hebrew root meaning "righteousness," "justice," or "fairness." In Judaism, giving to the poor is an act of justice and righteousness, the performance of duty, giving the poor their due.

LEVELS OF *TZEDAKAH*

The Talmud (historical Jewish commentaries) describes different levels of *tzedakah*. Moses Maimonides (1135–1204), known as the greatest Jewish philosopher, organized them into a list from the least to the most meritorious:

1. giving begrudgingly;
2. giving less that you should, but giving it cheerfully;
3. giving after being asked;
4. giving before being asked;
5. giving when you do not know the recipient's identity, but the recipient knows your identity;

6. giving when you know the recipient's identity, but the recipient doesn't know your identity;
7. giving when neither party knows the other's identity; and
8. enabling the recipient to become self-reliant.[1]

The apostle John reflected, "Whoever does not practice righteousness is not of God, nor *is* he who does not love his brother" (1 John 3:10).

Martin Buber, the famed Jewish scholar, echoed John's words when he wrote, "To love God truly, one must first love man. And if anyone tells you that he loves God and does not love his fellow-man, you will know that he is lying."[2]

---

1. Adapted from "Unveiling the 8 Degrees of Giving with Colel Chabad."
2. Buber, *Way of Man*, 99.

DAY 32

Mysterious Disasters—The Ninth Day of Av!

Tisha b'Av: the ninth day of the month of Av lands on Saturday evening, July 17.

The Jewish month of Av coincides with July and August. *Tisha B'Av* literally means "the ninth day of the Hebrew month of Av."

Mysterious and profound disasters happened on this date throughout the centuries. There are different theories as to why, from God's divine judgment upon Israel, to his sovereign order and rule of the universe, to the mysterious meanings of Hebrew letters, words, and holidays. Below is a list of some of the events that happened on the ninth day of Av.

1. The spies returned with a bad report (Num 13).
2. Both temples were destroyed (586 BC; AD 70).
3. The Bar Kokhba Revolt, also known as Bethar and the last Jewish stronghold, fell on the Ninth of Av, AD 135.
4. One year later, the Roman Emperor Hadrian set up a heathen temple on the site of the former Jewish Temple and rebuilt Jerusalem as a pagan city, refusing Jews to enter the Holy City.

5. The First Crusades in 1096 led to the destruction of Jewish communities in France and along the Rhine River.
6. Jews were expelled from England in 1290.
7. Also, on the ninth of Av, 1492, the Christian rulers of Spain expelled all the Jews from the land who lived there for centuries.
8. During World War II, the Holocaust, historians conclude, was the continuation of World War I that began in 1914. And yes, amazingly enough, Germany declared war on Russia, thus setting the First World War into motion on the ninth of Av, *Tisha b'Av*.
9. SS Commander Heinrich Himmler moved forward with the "Final Solution," which led to the destruction of one-third of world Jewry and the murder of six million Jews beginning in 1941.

THERE IS HOPE

This is not a time to simply reflect on the tragedies, but to be reminded that we should go forward to do what the Lord commands us to do. We need to pray for the coming of the messiah and work towards justice and peace. The vision of the prophet Isaiah tells us that the day will come when "nation shall not lift up sword against nation, neither shall they learn war anymore" (Isa 2:4).

The Lord will comfort his people (Isa 52:9), and he will make Jerusalem a delight and bless them in profound ways (Isa 60:15; 65:18, 19).

GOD RESTORES AND FORGIVES

If a person, church, city, or nation confesses their sins and returns to God, he will forgive, restore, and heal (2 Chr 7:14; 1 John 1:9).

Pray with our Jewish friends during this time of reflection. Pray that God will draw their hearts to him.

We continue to stand with and to pray for Israel during these last days. On one hand, Israel will experience more difficult days ahead. On the other hand, we are promised that Israel will experience in this day a "remnant" who will believe (Rom 11:5).

DAY 33

Don't Mess with Abraham

Blessing I will bless you, and multiplying I will multiply your descendants as the stars of the heaven and as the sand which is on the seashore. —Gen 22:17

Rabbis generally question these words by asking, "Would it have been better if the Torah said 'as the sand' or 'as the stars?'" They ask, "Why does the Torah use both?"

Their conclusion was that God revealed to Abraham a vision of his future progeny. He saw that they would be persecuted and downtrodden like the sand. But eventually, he would raise them up like the stars of the heavens.

God made a covenant with Abram ("exalted father"): his name would be changed to Abraham ("father of a multitude") in 17:1–8; that would change the world.

> I will make you a great nation;
> I will bless you
> And make your name great;
> And you shall be a blessing.
> I will bless those who bless you,
> And I will curse him who curses you;
> And in you all the families of the earth shall be blessed.
> (Gen 12:2–3)

Genesis 12:2-3 contains seven blessings. Seven is the number of perfection. The blessing that was bestowed upon Abraham was perfect.

1. "I will make you a great nation"
2. "I will bless you"
3. "And make your name great"
4. "And you shall be a blessing"
5. "I will bless those who bless you"
6. "And I will curse him who curses you"
7. "And in you all the families of the earth shall be blessed"

Abraham's sons, Isaac (Gen 26:3-4) and Jacob (Gen 27:28-29) received similar blessings.

1. ***A great nation:*** In old age, Abram was given the promise of an abundance of offspring. This was a promise that would test his faith.
2. ***I will bless you:*** Here the promise is regarding protection, peace, and a bestowal of all that is good, which would be highlighted some 430 years later by the Aaronic blessing found in Num 6:24-26 describing a life that is blessed by the Lord.
3. ***Make your name great:*** It is a promise that Abram's name would not only represent his personality, but it would be associated with the idea called Abraham and the impact his purpose and calling would have on the world. His name has great worth.
4. ***You shall be a blessing:*** The mysterious fruit of his great worth through the prophets, priests, kings, and ultimately the messiah will bless the nations beyond measure.
5. ***I will bless those who bless you:*** The word "bless" means to serve, the concept of bending the knee. When one bends the knee, it implies doing service for someone: to bring benefit,

to show sympathy, friendship, and/or seek their welfare, thus blessing the person (or in this case the people of Abraham through Isaac and Jacob).

6. *And I will curse him who curses you:* Those who would hurt, harm, or seek evil against Abraham will be cursed.

Two different Hebrew words are used for "curse." The first is *kalal*, meaning "to consider lightly," "to hold in contempt," "not taking them seriously"—a throw away. The second word is *aor*, which means "to absolutely destroy," "to annihilate," "to extinguish," "to end."

Simply put, God said to Abraham, "I will bless and do good by those who bless and do good by you. However, I will entirely destroy and outright end those who take you lightly or harm you!" For example, the Egyptians, Babylonians, Romans, and the German Third Reich who cursed Israel are empires in the dust.

7. *And in you all the families of the earth will be blessed:* Abraham's messianic seed will become the source of blessing to all nations. This blessing, or spiritual blessings, will extend to the gentiles as promised through the prophets (Isa 42:1, 6; 49:5, 6; Amos 9:11, 12).

We owe a great debt to the Jewish people. The Bible, prophets, priests, kings, and the messiah came through the Jews. Gentiles go to church because of the Jewish witness of Messiah to gentiles (Acts 10).

Simply put, "Bless the seed of Abraham," and do not "take [them] lightly." Don't mess with Abraham!

DAY 34

Problems and Solutions—From the Prophet Haggai!

With the Babylonian exile in the past and Jews returning to the land, work of rebuilding the temple began. However, the project was pushed aside as the people were putting their personal affairs first. Things began to happen to the nation. Economic problems unfolded and natural disasters began to happen. Let's find out what happened some 2500 years ago.

PROBLEM: FINANCIAL

Now therefore, thus says the LORD of hosts: "Consider your ways! You have sown much, and bring in little; You eat, but do not have enough; You drink, but you are not filled with drink; You clothe yourselves, but no one is warm; And he who earns wages, Earns wages to *put* into a bag with holes." (Hag 1:5–6)

PROBLEMS AND SOLUTIONS—FROM THE PROPHET HAGGAI!

SOLUTION: DO WHAT IS RIGHT—PUT THE LORD FIRST

"Consider your ways! Go up to the mountains and bring wood and build the temple, that I may take pleasure in it and be glorified," says the LORD. (Hag 1:7–8)

PROBLEM: NATURAL DISASTERS

"*You* looked for much, but indeed *it came to* little; and when you brought it home, I blew it away. Why?" says the LORD of hosts. "Because of My house that *is in* ruins, while every one of you runs to his own house. Therefore the heavens above you withhold the dew, and the earth withholds its fruit. For I called for a drought on the land and the mountains, on the grain and the new wine and the oil, on whatever the ground brings forth, on men and livestock, and on all the labor of *your* hands." (Hag 1:9–11)

SOLUTION: OBEDIENCE

Then Zerubbabel the son of Shealtiel, and Joshua the son of Jehozadak, the high priest, with all the remnant of the people, obeyed the voice of the LORD their God, and the words of Haggai the prophet, as the LORD their God had sent him; and the people feared the presence of the LORD. Then Haggai, the LORD's messenger, spoke the LORD's message to the people, saying, "I *am* with you, says the LORD." (Hag 1:12–13)

PROBLEM: DOESN'T LOOK THE SAME

Who is left among you who saw this temple in its former glory? And how do you see it now? In comparison with it, *is this* not in your eyes as nothing? (Hag 2:3)

SOLUTION: BE STRONG IN THE LORD

"'Be strong . . . be strong . . . be strong . . . for I am with you,' says the LORD of hosts. . . . 'My Spirit remains among you; do not fear!'" (Hag 2:4, 5)

ALL OF IT BELONGS TO THE LORD

For thus says the LORD of hosts: "Once more (it *is* a little while) I will shake heaven and earth, the sea and dry land; and I will shake all nations, and they shall come to the Desire of All Nations, and I will fill this temple with glory," says the LORD of hosts. "The silver *is* Mine, and the gold *is* Mine," says the LORD of hosts. (Hag 2:6–9)

NEVER FORGET

> And now, carefully consider from this day forward: from before stone was laid upon stone in the temple of the LORD . . . Is the seed still in the barn? As yet the vine, the fig tree, the pomegranate, and the olive tree have not yielded *fruit*. *But* from this day I will bless *you*. (Hag 2:15–19)

Nothing is new! Because of selfishness, sin, and pride, disasters, both economic and natural, fell upon Israel. Only when they repented, changed their ways, and trusted in the Lord did these calamities change. There were still scars—it didn't look the same. Nevertheless, God was with them, and basically he said to them, "Never forget what happened, where you came from and what I did for you! *I own it all; therefore, bow before me and do what is right!*"

Don't be afraid; God owns it all—trust in him and be obedient to his word!

DAY 35

Fear: *Yir'ah*

The fear of the Lord is the beginning of wisdom, And the knowledge of the Holy One is understanding. —Prov 9:10

Submitting to one another in the fear of God. —Eph 5:21

His delight is in the fear of the LORD. —Isa 11:3

By humility and *the fear of the* LORD *are riches and honor and life.* —Prov 22:4

Fear (Hebrew *yir'ah*) encompasses positive feelings such as honor, respect, reverence, and worshipful awe.

The "fear of the Lord" is a reverence for God that allows us to grow in intimate knowledge of him. It reassures us of his power and control over the world. It gives us a respect for his law that keeps us from sins which destroy our relationships and lives.

Yir'ah describes the sense of spine-tingling awe we have when we feel God's powerful presence—a sense God's overwhelming vastness worshipful wonder.

When someone shares a story of God's miraculous intervention in their lives, we are awed by God's power and personal care. In this sense, having "fear" of God is one of the most profound spiritual experiences of our lives.

To fear the Lord is the ultimate expression of knowing that we stand in the presence of a holy God. We are reminded that God is watching. We become reassured of his awesome power over this world, and as a result, we are comforted.

It can also mean to dread his disapproval of our sin, but the emphasis is on the reverential relationship with God, not on being afraid of him. The prophet said "Woe is me" as he saw the Lord "high and lifted up" in the temple. As he acknowledged his sin before the Lord, his life was changed forever, becoming an instrument whom God used in profound ways (Isa 6).

Having a healthy fear of the Lord will cause us to live with integrity and obedience to him; it will ultimately transform us.

> In the fear of the LORD *there is* strong confidence, And His children will have a place of refuge. The fear of the LORD *is* a fountain of life, To turn *one* away from the snares of death. (Prov 14:26–27)

DAY 36

Your Name

A name in Hebrew is like a book—in fact, a name is a book, a story of a person's character. The Hebrew word for name is "Shem" such as "HaShem" ("the name"). Religious Jews will not say "God" but rather "Adonai" or "HaShem."

In rabbinical thinking and in some circles of the church, someone's name describes that person's purpose, goal, or mission in life—like a prophetic blessing. Parents give this profound gift to their children; a name sets a course for the child.

GOD STARTED THIS

It was God who began naming things, and individuals. "God created" means he spoke the very words and that something or someone came into being.

When God said "let there be light" (or simply in Hebrew "light") and there was light, how did light know to be light? God named it, and its essence came into being—the power of a name.

ABRAM

When Abram came to the clear understanding that there was only one God, his name had to be changed: "No longer shall your name be called Abram, but your name shall be Abraham; for I have made you a father of many nations" (Gen 17:5). The son of a pagan is now the father of many nations who will follow God.

JACOB

Jacob's name means "heel," implying a characteristic of running away from life's challenges. He was a sensitive soul who found himself in a situation where he had to stand and fight, taking a risk and not fleeing from the challenge facing him. And God said, "Your name shall no longer be called Jacob, but Israel; for you have struggled with God and with men, and have prevailed"(Gen. 32:28). A painful life experience changes people. Jacob, who was afraid and fled, now limps with purpose and determination.

> For as his name *is*, so *is* he. (1 Sam 25:25)

OTHERS

In the New Testament, Peter's name was changed, reflecting his faith in Messiah. Paul had two names. Those who believe in Messiah Jesus become a new creature and will be given a new name: "And the disciples were first called Christians in Antioch" (Acts 11:26). This means they were "Messiah-like." They so resembled Jesus the Messiah, they were called "Messiah-like."

YOUR PATH

A name is a statement of the person's character and path in life. If God named creation and the stars (Gen 1; Ps 147:4) and he gave man the task of naming animals, how much more should parents prayerfully choose the names of their children?

Granted, we all have free will and can choose our path—even if our names do not reflect our journey. However, parents can do the right thing and encourage their children's journey by giving them names with meaning.

OUR NAME

Children in the war zones of the Middle East need adults to do the right thing as well. In the region, our name "Israel Today Ministries" means God's people are blessing the children of Abraham (both Jews and Arabs). Help us bless the children and survivors in Israel by your prayers and loving generosity. Contact Israel Today Ministries, israeltodayministries.org

DAY 37

Messed Up!

SECOND PASSOVER

God is a God of second chances. For example, *Peseach Sheni* means "Second Passover." One year after the exodus, God instructed the people of Israel to celebrate Passover on the fourteenth day of Nissan (springtime): to bring an offering and to reenact the eating of the various foods as they had done the previous year, thus recalling their exodus from Egypt.

However, there were those who had become ritually impure through contact with a dead body, and as a result, they were unable to prepare the Passover offering that day. So they appealed to Moses for a solution. As a result of their plea, God inaugurated a second chance to bring an offering and celebrate Passover the following month, on the fourteenth day of Iyar, called *Pesach Sheni* or "Second Passover" (Num 9:1–14).

This day gave those who "messed up" a chance to repent (Hebrew *teshuvah*), to return in obedience.

JONAH

God told Jonah to go to Nineveh and proclaim the word of repentance. Jonah purchased a ticket to sail not to Nineveh, but rather to flee from the presence of the Lord, heading towards Tarshish. Apparently, he thought the Lord would not find him there.

As the records states, "The LORD sent out a great wind on the sea, and there was a mighty tempest on the sea" (Jonah 1:4). Jonah fell asleep while the crew panicked. Realizing this calamity was a result of Jonah's disobedience, they threw him overboard and a great fish swallowed him, eventually vomiting the noncompliant man of God onto dry ground.

Then "the word of the LORD came to Jonah the second time" (3:1). There it is. God is a God of second chances. Jonah did repent and fulfilled his calling, though reluctantly.

The Bible has many stories of second chances. The point is to remind us that when we are disobedient and "mess it up," the sun will come up in the morning, and God will give us a second chance to be obedient to his calling upon our lives (Lam 3:20–24).

POINTS TO PONDER

1. Second chances never run out—only time runs out.
2. Take notice of every moment in your life that God has given you a second chance. Then praise him!
3. Don't waste a second chance God gives you.
4. Your life is not so "messed up" that God can't restore you, forgive you, and help you with a second chance. He is able. "For I, the LORD your God, will hold your right hand, Saying to you, 'Fear not, I will help you'" (Isa 41:13).

DAY 38

Does God Care?

This past year we have found ourselves ministering to those in Israel who have suffered greatly during this war of October 7, 2023. The horror, the evil brutality is beyond words.

Because of the stress and fear, the children wet their beds and rock back and forth while sitting, not even realizing they are doing this motion. The children have nightmares; parents weep and struggle because of grief and loss of loved ones either kidnapped or killed. The PTSD has affected everyone.

In circumstances like this, the question is often asked, "Does God care?" The early church fathers, both Latin and Greek, insisted upon what is called the "impassibility" of God. Basically, this means that while man experiences suffering, God himself does not. Yet, portions of the Hebrew Scripture narrative imply God does have feelings and does react to suffering and pain.

We find it stated of God:

> His soul could no longer endure the misery of Israel. (Judg 10:16)

> *Is* Ephraim My dear son? *Is* he a pleasant child? For though I spoke against him, I earnestly remember him still; therefore My heart yearns for him; I will surely have mercy on him, says the LORD. (Jer 31:20)

> How can I give you up, Ephraim? *How* can I hand you over, Israel? How can I make you like Admah? *How* can I set you like Zeboiim? My heart churns within Me; My sympathy is stirred. (Hos 11:8)

It is stated of Messiah:

> And when He came near the gate of the city, behold, a dead man was being carried out, the only son of his mother; and she was a widow.... When the Lord saw her, He had compassion on her and said to her, "Do not weep." (Luke 7:12–13)

> Therefore, when Jesus saw her weeping, and the Jews who came with her weeping, He groaned in the spirit and was troubled.... Jesus wept. Then the Jews said, "See how He loved him!" (John 11:33–36)

> But when He saw the multitudes He was moved with compassion. (Matt 9:36)

Looking at these passages, if we learn anything at all, we learn that God is directly affected by the trials and anguish, identifying with human pain and responding with immeasurable love.

GOD CARES

Our suffering causes God to grieve. God cries when we cry; God hurts when we hurt. This of course does not diminish who God is in terms of his essence, being all power, all knowledge, everywhere present. If human beings, created in God's image, can make suffering their own through their love for others, how much more can God, who is love, make our suffering his own?

In other words, if a human is affected by another's sorrow and pain, God is more affected. Why? God created us out of an act of love, and is not indifferent to the angst we experience. He created us and is involved and identifies with us—even proving his involvement by taking it to the ultimate expression of love and concern: the cross.

Simply, God cries when someone dies; he has compassion on those who are ill; he sorrows for the children who do not have a meal; his heart yearns for the one gone astray; he has sympathy for those in need.

Our sorrow is mingled with joy because Messiah brings hope and answers in our time of need. God expressed his love through the life, death, and resurrection of Messiah Jesus. The resurrection proves that he is God. God is not indifferent to the sorrows of this world—and that brings an amazing comfort to my heart. "Weeping may endure for a night, but joy *comes* in the morning" (Ps 30:5).

DAY 39

Grandma's Prayer

"YOU ARE THE FIRST"

Grandma would disappear every evening after dinner. As a child, I thought she was taking a nap—after all, that's what grandmas do, or so I thought.

After I became a Christian, the first person I told about my experience was my grandmother. With a tear in her eye, she said, "Oh Jeffrey, let me show you something." She led me to her room, opened the credenza, and pulled out the drawer. She lifted an old, tattered, yellowed notebook full of names and dates. Grandma flipped through the pages until she found my name. She put a check mark beside my name and dated it. She said, "You are the first in your family to become a Christian. Jeffrey, I have been praying for you for eighteen years."

Grandma wasn't sleeping after dinner; she was praying. She prayed faithfully every day, as much as she could, for her family and loved ones. Recently, my eighty-one-year-old Aunt Dorothy in Florida told me a story about how Grandma could no longer climb the stairs and would simply live on the main floor of her home, sleeping on a cot. While staying with her for a week, my aunt observed each evening Grandma struggling to get on her knees to pray—and, indeed, she made it to the floor and prayed. My grandmother was old-school determined. What a beautiful legacy! Grandma is in heaven now experiencing the wonder of eternal life.

WATCHING OVER US

Prayers do work. My wife Louise and I have received emails and notes from people who have prayed for us at a certain time and a certain hour. We would discover that they were praying when we were in a precarious situation in some village in the Middle East. God knew we needed protection, and he answered their prayers and watched over us.

"PRAYER CHANGES ME"

The Hebrew word for prayer is *tefilah*. It comes from a word meaning "to judge oneself." The most important part of prayer, whether it is a prayer of petition, of thanksgiving, of praise of God, or of confession, is the introspection, self-analysis, soul-searching, or simply the self-examination it provides regarding our lives and our relationships to God.

DIVINE

The Yiddish word for "pray" is *daven*, which comes from the Latin meaning "divine," thus emphasizing the one to whom prayer is directed.

Some people pray when inspired or motivated by tragedy. However, to set aside a regular routine of prayer is difficult for many.

MINDSET

We can look at it this way: when a person prays regularly, it is not just an act of petition; rather, it is an act of worship. We need to change our mindset—this is not an act of duty, but an act of relationship.

PRACTICE

Prayer can develop your awareness of God's presence. Like anything else you do, you need to practice.

An athlete will go over the routines until it hurts. When the day of the game arrives, the athlete is in the "zone," and there is great gratification.

A couple who date and play together and communicate together find fulfillment. A parent who spends time with their children, unplugging, not answering the phone, dedicating the moment for the sake of enhancing their relationship with their little ones, teenagers, or young adults will find it rewarding.

When you pray, maybe light candles or close the door, shut off the light, or find a special spot outdoors/indoors and have a date with God, dedicating the moment to enhance your relationship with him. Talk to him (he talks to you), play with God, have fun with him, communicate with him, give God your love, and allow God to love you. Then perhaps, after all this practice, you will become fully aware of God's presence as you lay bare, completely transparent and vulnerable, and you will tremble with holy fear and awe because you begin to realize, as Isaiah stated, "Woe is me, for I am undone! Because I am a man of unclean lips," a sinful creature, and yet you will discover God's forgiveness, love, and embrace because of the blood of the Lamb of God, Jesus, who died on the cross and rose again the third day.

I DON'T KNOW HOW

You may say, "I don't know what to pray." In traditional Judaism, praying in Hebrew is preferred. One man did not know Hebrew; however, he knew the Hebrew alphabet. So he prayed the alphabet in Hebrew over and over again, routinely, day after day.

A rabbi asked, "Why do you pray the alphabet?"

The man told the rabbi, "The Holy One, blessed is he, knows what is in my heart. I will give him the letters, and he can put the words together."

SHE PRACTICED

Every night my grandma got on her knees, even when her knees hurt. She practiced prayer. Prayer changed her. God enabled her to change things and, because she had an awareness of and relationship with God, he heard her prayers and did the miraculous—those things that only God can do.

So, beloved, let's attempt to practice prayer, and in so doing develop a closer relationship with God and experience the celestial.

> Call to Me, and I will answer you, and show you great and mighty things, which you do not know. (Jer 33:3)

> He has put a new song in my mouth. (Ps 40:3)[1]

---

1. Why did David say this? He prayed to God!

DAY 40

God Declares

I often quote to encourage those who are in a vortex of fear and anxiety, "For I, the LORD your God, will hold your right hand, Saying to you, 'Fear not, I will help you'" (Isa 41:13). It is a great verse! When you read this verse in context regarding what is written before and what is written after, you appreciate the verse a little more.

CONFRONTING NATIONS

The Lord confronted the nations and reminded them that he is in control of history, not them. God raises up kings and he also topples them—he is absolutely sovereign over world events. Cyrus, God's anointed shepherd and the Persian emperor, was coming to overthrow Babylon, and the nations could do nothing against the Persian "shepherd"—God had so declared it to be (Isa 41:1-7; 44:28—45:1-4).

I WILL NOT ABANDON

God reminds Israel that he chose them and Abraham was his friend. He brought them back from Babylonian captivity and said to them, "You *are* My servant . . . I have chosen you and have not cast you away" (Isa 41:8, 9). God did not abandon Israel.

WILL BECOME NOTHING

God continues to reassure his people Israel not to fear or be anxious, that he will strengthen and help them. The Lord said all those who are angry at you (Israel) and contend with you will be dishonored; and those who quarrel and war with you will become nothing (Isa 41:10–12).

Then he declares, "For I, the Lord your God, will hold your right hand, Saying to you, 'Fear not, I will help you'" (Isa 41:13).

LIKE A PARENT

As challenges seem great and uncertainty abounds, remember, God declares, like a parent, he holds your right hand and says, "Fear not, I will help you."

KINGS COME, KINGS GO

Regarding events of the world, remember God is sovereign—he raises kings up, and he can topple them (Isa 41–45; Rom 13). Our job is to pray and vote—God will do the rest.

Beloved, may we be comforted by what the prophet penned in chapters 41–45 of Isaiah. Read the chapters and let God speak to you and comfort you. What he did for Israel, he will do for you. They were released from captivity and were able to go back to Jerusalem to rebuild their broken temple.

POINTS TO PONDER

1. God is sovereign over world events.
2. God chose you as he chose Abraham (John 15:16).
3. Abraham was God's friend—and so are you (John 15:14).
4. God will not abandon you.
5. God created you and thinks about you (Ps 40:17).

GOD DECLARES

6. God raises kings up and he can topple them (Rom 13).
7. God promised to hold your hand and help you.
8. There is no need to fear.

DAY 41

Yes Be Yes!

Jesus said,

> Again you have heard that it was said to those of old, "You shall not swear falsely, but shall perform your oaths to the Lord." But I say to you, do not swear at all: neither by heaven, for it is God's throne; nor by the earth, for it is His footstool; nor by Jerusalem, for it is the city of the great King. Nor shall you swear by your head, because you cannot make one hair white or black. But let your "Yes" be "Yes," and your "No," "No." For whatever is more than these is from the evil one. (Matt 5:33–37)

Here Jesus was speaking to things such as bartering. Buying and selling is a complicated business in the Middle East. Bargaining or bartering is a way of life.

For example, one would say, "By God's name and his holy angels, this pair of shoes cost me six dollars, but you can have it for three dollars," or, "By my only son's head, I cannot pay you more than a dollar." Jesus said don't swear or make a vow like this.

Jesus responded to an oath, as did Paul, by saying that *one's life should be sufficient* to back up one's words (Matt 26:63, 64; 2 Cor 1:23). Your integrity should speak volumes. Our "yes" should be "yes" and our "no" should be "no."

James emphasized the Lord's words in his epistle: "But above all, my brethren, do not swear, either by heaven or by earth or with any other oath. But let your 'Yes' be 'Yes,' and *your* 'No,' 'No,' lest you fall into judgment" (Jas 5:12).

Israelis will hear about what you do before they hear what you say. In other words, your actions speak louder than your words. During the pandemic and recent war, Israel Today Ministries continued to supply needed food for children and survivors. I personally told each organization that we work with, "We stand with you." And when the pandemic paralyzed the world, we continued providing food. When the war shattered Israeli society, we continued providing food. Our "yes" was "yes."

DAY 42

Six Things to Remember About God's Silence

Being a Christian, a follower of God, does not mean that you will be trouble-free. In every case, the believer experienced obstacles and valleys, and sometimes it cost them their lives. Months, years, decades—God speaks, and it is then clear regarding the question "Why?"

It seems to me that the propensity of God is to be silent. It is an act of grace and love. His silence strengthens our faith. "Faith is the substance of things hoped for, the evidence of things not seen" (Heb 11:1).

Is God there? Yes! He is Emmanuel, "God with us." You can see him in the surreal universe (Ps 19:1). You can see him in the gift of children (Luke 18:15–17). He is there in every breath you take (Acts 17:25). Every changed life is a testimony to the fact that God is there (2 Cor 5:17). Every miracle points us to God (Luke 1:37).

Sometimes we cannot see because our hearts are not clean. When we humble our hearts before him, seek him, and confess our sin, he will cleanse our hearts, and we will see him (Heb 12:14; 1 John 1:8–10). To seek the path of peace, holiness, and love is a difficult road. It is not natural for human beings to do so. It is only through his Spirit, seeking to follow his Christ, that we shall see God, for Christ is God (1 John 4:4; Heb 11:6).

POINTS TO PONDER

1. Therefore beloved, when God is silent, remember he *is* there. He promised he will never leave nor forsake us (Heb 13:5).
2. When God is silent, it is an act of grace and love to strengthen our faith (Heb 11:1).
3. When God is silent, he has a greater purpose in mind, though we may not fully understand (Rom 8:28–39).
4. When God is silent, the Spirit will make intercession for us, for we do not know what to pray (Rom 8:26–27).
5. When God is silent, we are to wait and hope for that which we do not see, nor understand (Rom 8:24–25; Isa 40:31).
6. When God is silent, do not despair, for at the exact moment, when the time is right, he will speak, and you will know what it means to seek him.

Shall not the Judge of all the earth do right? (Gen 18:25)

Blessed *be* the LORD God of Israel from everlasting to everlasting! And all the people said, "Amen!" and praised the LORD. (1 Chr 16:36)

DAY 43

Your Work Continues!

Concerning the afterlife, the apostle John writes, "Beloved, now we are children of God; and it has not yet been revealed what we shall be, but we know that when He is revealed, we shall be like Him, for we shall see Him as He is" (1 John 3:2). From the very beginning believers looked forward to life everlasting.

Heaven is real, and yet, much of heaven remains a mystery, and mystery is good, for "eye has not seen, nor ear heard, nor have entered into the heart of man the things which God has prepared for those who love Him" (1 Cor 2:9). Heaven is more than anything we could ever imagine.

It is amazing to know that heaven is real and is promised by Jesus himself, for he said, "All that the Father gives Me will come to Me, and the one who comes to Me I will by no means cast out. . . . This is the will of the Father who sent Me, that of all He has given Me I should lose nothing, but should raise it up at the last day" (John 6:37, 39).

Jesus, speaking to Martha after her brother Lazarus had died, said to her lovingly, "Your brother will rise again. . . . I am the resurrection and the life. He who believes in Me, though he may die, he shall live. And whoever lives and believes in Me shall never die. Do you believe this?" (John 11:23, 25–26).

At times, Jesus spoke in symbols and metaphors regarding the hope for those who believe in him. In John 14:1–3 and Luke

14:15–24, the Lord gives us brief glimpses of the reassurance of life after death. Within verses like these, we find brief glimpses of their ultimate truth giving us reassurance of life after death.

The apostle John writes, "And I heard a loud voice from heaven saying, 'Behold, the tabernacle of God *is* with men, and He will dwell with them, and they shall be His people. God Himself will be with them *and be* their God. And God will wipe away every tear from their eyes; there shall be no more death, nor sorrow, nor crying. There shall be no more pain, for the former things have passed away'"(Rev 21:3–4).

Heaven is a closeness with God. Heaven is not static, for John states "[our] works will follow [us]" in the afterlife and that we will "rest" (Rev 14:13). The word "rest" has the idea of freedom from weakness, failure, and the limitations we currently have in our bodies.

In other words, we shall continue to be productive without the fragility of becoming tired or pausing, reinforcing the principle of moving straight ahead, that of progressive activity.

Christ tells us that there will be the reward of more responsibility and gratification of self-worth (Matt 24:45–47; 25:20–23; Luke 19:15–19). To the great will be given great and to the small will be given small—all will have worth and responsibility within the kingdom. This means that our life work here is a preparation for bigger, ongoing work there. Jesus puts it plainly when he states, "My Father has been working until now, and I have been working" (John 5:17). He also said, "I say to you, he who believes in Me, the works that I do he will do also; and greater *works* than these he will do" (John 14:12).

Death is swallowed up in the victory through our Lord Jesus Christ (1 Cor 15:54, 57). "For now we see in a mirror, dimly, but then face to face. Now I know in part, but then I shall know just as I also am known" (1 Cor 13:12).

The things we believe by faith we now hear on the authority of the Scriptures. One day we will know them in reality when partial knowledge has ceased. "Face to face" means with absolute clarity and luminescence. In heaven, we shall completely understand all the mysteries and questions we have in this life. "Wherever we shall turn the eyes of our spiritual bodies we shall see the immaterial God, ruling all things, and we shall see him by means of our bodies," said Augustine about heaven.[1] What a wonderful hope followers in Jesus possess!

---

1. Augustine, *City of God*, 504.

DAY 44

Mystery of the Olive Tree

SYMBOLS

The olive tree is a symbol of Israel. Olive trees appear in the emblems of both the State of Israel, as well as the Israeli Defense Forces (IDF).

The olive tree is also a symbol of peace, hope, and many other qualities that are important to Israel and the Jewish people.

STRIKING

In biblical times, olives were harvested by beating the branches of the tree with sticks to make the olives fall, which were then collected in a basket to be pressed to extract the oil.

The oil produced from the olives was used for cooking, lighting, medicinal purposes, and moisturizing skin. It was also used as an important part of the worship of God and was a symbol of immense blessing in Scripture. The Bible mentions the olive harvest in Isa 17:6 and Deut 24:20. The Hebrew term *noqeph zayit* appears in Isa 17:6, which means "a beater of olives." *Noqeph* means "to strike," "to go around and around shaking and striking". *Zayit* means "olives." To harvest the fruit, the tree needed to be struck, to be traumatized, to experience trouble, pain, and difficulty again and again as it was shaken and beaten. You could not eat the olive off the tree as it was bitter to the taste. The olives needed to be pressed and processed to produce oil for cooking, light, medicine, and general healing.

SUFFERING

This is a powerful metaphor for Israel as well as the church. Israel has experienced trauma for millennia, and Jesus implied that if you want to follow him, it will cost you (Luke 14:25–35). Paul said believers will suffer for Christ (Phil 1:29; 3:10; 2 Tim 3:12).

SPIRITUALITY

Olive trees are evergreen. They keep their leaves year-round. This is symbolic of God's everlasting covering. God protects and provides as he watches over his people (Ps 91). However, when we experience trouble or pain being struck by life's challenges, he watches over us and produces fruit in us. Israel's fruit bore the revelation of Messiah to the world and eventually will experience a complete national restoration and revival, coming to faith in Messiah Yeshua.

For the follower of Jesus, olive oil is also a symbol of the *Ruach HaKodesh*—the Holy Spirit. Believers have God the Holy Spirit within them who convicts, comforts, guides, reveals Jesus, and produces fruit (John 16:5–15; Gal 5:22, 23). Though we may suffer for a little while, God will restore, support, and strengthen you, placing you on a firm foundation under his covering (1 Pet 5:10). The olive tree reminds us of these things.

DAY 45

The One Worthy

John is the most mystical of the Gospel writers. His communication emphasizes the otherworldliness of Jesus.

In his opening statement of his Gospel, he writes, "In the beginning was the Word, and the Word was with God, and the Word was God" (John 1:1).

He uses the Greek word *pros*, translated "with," which implies the "Word" was interfacing with and of the same essence as God. Then he says "the Word was God," which is written properly in English with the subject *before* the predicate. The subject is the word "Word"; the predicate is the word "God."

However, in Greek, the predicate in this sentence is *first* for emphasis: *Theos en ho logos*—"God was the Word." "And the Word [who is God] became flesh [who is Jesus]" (v. 14).

REACTION

The fact that Jesus is God was made clear by the reaction of the disciples in the boat rowing for their lives. As the disciples were to the point of complete fatigue, watching the waves and swells go up and down crashing into their tiny boat, they saw something in the dark, early in the morning before sunrise. *"Look! There is an object in the water—no, wait, it is on top of the water—it is a man, no, it is a ghost—what is that? Lord, is that really you?"*

Jesus was walking on top of the waves, stepping over them like one would step over rocks. He was not in the water but on top of the waves and swells. He was about to walk "past" them (Mark 6:48).

"Do not be afraid!" said Jesus. And then, after Peter also walked on the water, Jesus climbed into the boat (Matt 14:28, 32). The storm ceased and the disciples worshiped him (literally "prostrated themselves before"), saying, "Truly you are the Son of God" (Matt 14:33).

THEY "WORSHIPED"

Judaism doesn't allow the worship of a man—no matter how religious. This is a major turning point in history as the disciples began to understand there is something more profound about this man named Jesus (*Yeshua*). He is more than a king and more than a political messiah. He is bigger than all these human expectations. Who is this man who walks on water? Soon they would understand that he is God in the flesh.

John's account of the story tells us that when they were willing to take him into the boat, "immediately" they reached their destination on shore where they were heading (John 6:21).

Perhaps the disciples thought of Moses when Jesus said, "It is I; do not be afraid"(John 6:20). Moses said to Israel trapped in front of the Red Sea, "'Do not be afraid. Stand still [firm], and [you will] see the salvation [*Yeshua*, Jesus] of the LORD . . . today'" (Exod 14:13). Jesus's name in Hebrew is *Yeshua*, meaning "salvation" or "deliverance."

Job stated,

> He [God] alone spreads out the heavens, And treads on the waves of the sea; He made the Bear, Orion, and the Pleiades, And the chambers [constellations] of the south; He does great things past finding out, Yes, wonders

without number. If He goes by me, I do not see *Him*; If
He moves past, I do not perceive Him. (Job 9:8–11)

Paul stated that Jesus is God, and "by Him all things were created" (Col 1:16). From the apostle John to Paul, we are told that it was Jesus, before the beginning, who was with God, who was God, and became flesh, who is the one who created the heavens and earth, the one who walks on water and calms the waves, and is the one worthy of our worship and praise.

DAY 46

The Right Thing to Do!

Surely He shall deliver you from the snare of the fowler And from the perilous pestilence.
He shall cover you with His feathers, And under His wings you shall take refuge; His truth shall be your shield and buckler. You shall not be afraid of the terror by night, Nor of the arrow that flies by day, Nor of the pestilence that walks in darkness,
Nor of the destruction that lays waste at noonday.
A thousand may fall at your side, And ten thousand at your right hand; But it shall not come near you.
Only with your eyes shall you look, And see the reward of the wicked. —Ps 91:3–8

In these verses, we are reminded that God's protection is an encompassing shield and wall wherein the presence of God dwells and is where you find safety and peace. God protects us in the darkness, where there is no light, and at noon, when the brightest of the light shines.

Below are a couple of episodes in my life that taught me these mysterious and invaluable truths of God's love and protection. May God, the Holy Spirit, encourage, strengthen, and empower as you ponder these stories!

ENEMIES

In a Palestinian area, I was visiting with Arabs who believed in Jesus. This congregation of believers was amid a hoard of fundamentalist Muslims who did not want their Christian presence in the neighborhood.

I had opportunity to worship with them. On that Sunday, Brother Andrew was the speaker. Brother Andrew is of *God's Smuggler* fame. (If you have not read the book *God's Smuggler*, I strongly recommend you do.)

Before introducing Brother Andrew, Pastor Alex led us in prayer. He prayed for members of his congregation, community, nations, and then lightning struck in my ears as he prayed for the salvation of Yasser Arafat.

Wait a minute: Arafat was leader of the PLO at that time—our enemy. Oh, how the Holy Spirit pricked my heart. I have not prayed for the enemies of Israel or America. Anyway, timed passed and I forgot about the Holy Spirit pressing my heart.

A few years later, I was worshiping in our Jewish congregation in Jerusalem. Hamas was just "elected" into power in the Gaza Strip. Our teacher, Yossi, led us in prayer. Yes, he also prayed for our congregation, community, nations, and—you've guessed it—for Ismail Haniyeh, the senior leader of Hamas; he prayed for his salvation. Boom! Once again, the Holy Spirit pounded my heart about praying for those who are enemies or those with whom I disagree.

God is still working on me, and there are days that I do this better. I share this with you to encourage you to pray for those who may be your enemies or those with whom you disagree.

Jesus had a lot to say about such things:

> But I say to you, love your enemies, bless those who curse you, do good to those who hate you, and pray for those who spitefully use you and persecute you. (Matt 5:44)

Believers in Israel are surrounded by enemies. Rockets still fall from the sky and terrorists still plan attacks. Both Pastor Alex and Yossi exemplified how a believer is to react regarding those who try to harm you.

Let's heed Jesus's exhortation. It is truly the believer's privilege, responsibility, and duty to pray for our king (a discussion for another time), our enemies, and for those with whom we disagree. It is the right thing to do.

DAY 47

Very Personal

Psalm 139 is very personal. David paints for us the intimacy he feels toward God. There is a depth here, understanding the miracle and comfort of God's absolute sovereignty. In verse 13, David walks us through the mystery of God's mastery over the gestation process of life itself:

> For You formed my inward parts; You covered [wove] me in my mother's womb. (Ps 139:13)

"Formed" (Hebrew *kanita*) implies something originating from God.

David comprehended God's cause and effect. He was saying, "You, God, have created. This is something that only you can do. Only you can make through divine action someone from the mysterious substance of procreation."

"My inward parts" (Hebrew *chilyotai*), literally "of a physical organ," is often translated "kidney," which is a Middle Eastern way of saying "heart."

In the West we say, "I love you with all my heart." What we are actually implying is, "I love you with my whole being, every part of me." In the Middle East one may say, "I love you with all my 'kidney.'"

David contemplated, "You formed my heart, or my emotions, my affections, and my conscience. You have created my mind. Therefore, my thoughts do not surprise you. I am the way that I am, O Lord, for you have made me this way. I am 'wired' in a certain manner. I am unique, created in your image."

"Covered [Wove]" (Hebrew *tesukkeni*) means "you have covered" me or "lay over" me, you who "knits" or "weaves together." You "joined together" and "fashioned" me.

David considered, "Lord, you have created me part by part. You have knitted me and protected me through the gestation process. You wove together and created my embryo. You know every part of me. Nothing is hidden from you. You made me exactly the way I am. I am a miracle created by your holy design. I have significance."

"Womb" (Heb. *beveten*) means "in the womb of my mother." David understood, "I was part of her body, and yet it was my body, her blood, my blood, her flesh, my flesh. You have woven together bone and flesh. You have created my soul within my mother's womb. You saw me and knew me even in her womb. You are everywhere present, all-knowing, and all-powerful."

POINTS TO PONDER

1. God knew you would be alive at this hour.
2. God fashioned you, giving you the ability to face life challenges that you may be experiencing.
3. You are no mistake—God makes no mistakes!
4. Each day, we start anew.
5. Each morning we can renew our commitment to the Lord (Lam 3:22, 23).
6. God will provide (*YHVH-Jireh*) and God is almighty (*El-Shaddai*).

DAY 48

Scars and Circumstances

Recently, I was reminded of a story found in Judg 11 about a mighty man of valor, Jephthah.

We all have scars in life and circumstances that seemingly paralyze our purpose. God is bigger than our circumstances and dysfunctions. Let's begin.

JUDGES 11:1-11

Verse 1: Jephthah was a mighty man of valor, a military hero. His father was Gilead. However, his mother was a prostitute. There was a Sumerian law (Lipit-Ishtar) at that time which allowed a man who had no sons by his wife to have a son by a harlot, and that son could inherit his estate. Whether Israel had such a law is questionable.

Verse 2: Gilead, Jephthah's father, had a wife who bore him sons afterward. When they grew up, they realized that Jephthah was the firstborn; thus, he would receive an inheritance. They drove him away from the family because his mother was a whore, and the sons did not want him to receive any inheritance. It was all about money.

Verse 3: Jephthah fled to the land of Tob, northeast of Gilead, a place of lawbreakers and banished people, and associated himself with ruthless men who raided and pillaged.

Verse 4: Ammon declares war against Israel.

Verse 5: The elders of Gilead, desperate, went to get Jephthah from the land of Tob.

Verse 6: The elders offered him the position of commander (Hebrew *katzin*, "a man of war," "a magistrate," "leader," "chief") over Gilead as he was a mighty man of valor. They wanted his leadership and influence to lead a military campaign against the Ammonites.

Verse 7: Jephthah said to the elders, "You expelled me, and you did not stop my brothers, and you assisted in driving me out from my father's house. Now you want me back because you are in trouble and need my help?"

Verse 8: The elders did not deny the accusation, and said, "Yes, we need your help. We will make you commander [Hebrew *ro'sh*, 'head'] over all of Gilead."

Verse 9: Jephthah wanted to verify that if he leads the army to victory, they would make him head (Hebrew *ro'sh*) over Gilead.

Verse 10: The elders said, "Yes, absolutely!"

Verse 11: Jephthah went with the elders to Gilead, and in some religious ceremony before the Lord, most likely, had the elders repeat their words before the Lord, and in turn, Jephthah, before the Lord, accepted the terms. This would have been done in a place sanctified to the Lord, such as an altar or a pillar in the sanctuary or at a high place in Mizpah, which is the name of a couple of cities mentioned in Scripture. "Mizpah" means "watchtower" or "lookout" and is first mentioned in the Bible in Gen 31:45–49, which was located in Gilead in the mountains east of the Jordan River.

HOW DO THESE VERSES HELP YOU AND ME?

Verse 1: Jephthah was considered an illegitimate son of a whore and would have been looked down upon by his community. It is not specified, but somehow, he rose above his circumstances and became a military hero. By the way, there are no illegitimate children—only illegitimate parents. The child had nothing to do with being born. Jephthah's father decided to have intimate relations with the prostitute, the mother of Jephthah. Jephthah was innocent. Society labeled Jephthah as illegitimate.

Verse 2: A dysfunctional family dynamic unfolded through the years. Jephthah had stepbrothers who were jealous of him receiving an inheritance from their father. Therefore, they drove him away. Family rejected Jephthah.

Verse 3: Being rejected by his family, Jephthah fled, and as is anyone who is rejected by family, he became angry, and in his case, he joined with hoodlums pillaging everywhere they traveled. Jephthah rebelled in anger.

Verses 4-6: War is declared back home against Israel, and the elders (the spiritual leaders) who assisted in the expelling of Jephthah reached out to him for help. The hypocrisy of these men is profound. Spiritual leaders rejected and failed Jephthah.

Verses 7-11: Rejected and scorned by the elders, Jephthah naturally does not trust them. Therefore, he verifies their words before the Lord. Jephthah trusts but verifies.

The rest of the chapter is full of victory and tragedy.

THE POINT

It doesn't matter the circumstances against you—society, family, spiritual leaders, or mistakes you have made. God can use your dysfunctions and circumstances for his purposes. Rising above his circumstances, Jephthah became very successful, only to have it all ripped from him because of jealous family members. Rejected by those whom he trusted, he became angry and destructive, losing his way.

But then the elders came, and "the Spirit of the LORD came upon Jephthah" (v. 29). Like with Jonah, "the LORD came the second time" (Jonah 3:1).

God is a God of second chances. He can do the impossible. Trust him. He will lift you up in his timing, not yours. The "elders" will come, and the door will open, and your life will be changed. He's able to use you and your circumstances and to do things you never thought possible. He will come a second time.

DAY 49

Discovering Your Purpose, *Shema*!

"Hear, O Israel: The LORD our God, the LORD is one!"
—Deut 6:4[1]

Deuteronomy 6:4 is the beginning of what is called the *Shema* which is the heart of biblical Judaism. *Shema* means to "hear" and is prayed once in the morning and once in the evening, "when you lie down, and when you rise up" (Deut 6:7). It is recited when the Torah is taken out of the ark, which contains the Torah scroll; on Shabbat; during Holy Days; festivals; and on one's deathbed. Parchments of the *Shema* are found in the tefillin (boxes/leather straps on the left arm and forehead) and in the *mezuzahs* found on the doorposts of Jewish homes. Parents are to teach their children the *Shema* (Deut 6:1–9).

Shema doesn't only mean hearing with your ears; it has a deeper implication, that of hearing within one's innermost being, within your heart and soul. It is grasping the depth of God's oneness: "Oh, the depth of the riches both of the wisdom and knowledge of God! How unsearchable *are* His judgments and His ways past finding out!" (Rom 11:33). When "hearing" within one's deepest essence, you discover God and your purpose in the world.

---

1. Hebrew *Shema Yisrael, Adonai Eloheinu, Adonai echad.*

DISCOVERING YOUR PURPOSE, SHEMA!

When the Israelites received the Torah on Mount Sinai, they asserted, "All that the LORD has said we will do [*aseh*—'to do or make'] and be obedient [*shema*—'we will hear']" (Exod 24:7). *It is natural* for a believer to want "to do" first before understanding the meaning or purpose of the "hearing." *Even the angels* "do" before understanding the meaning or purpose of "hearing": "Bless the LORD, you His angels, Who excel in strength, who do [*aseh*—'to do or make'] His word, heeding [*shema*, 'to hear,' 'to obey'] the voice of His word" (Ps 103:20).

The rabbis say the letters of the *Shema* (Shin, Mem, and Ayin) backward are the first letters of the words *ol malchut shamayin* or "the yoke of the kingdom of Heaven," which means a horse or an ox who wears a yoke in the plowing of a field. The objective is to plant seed and yield a bountiful harvest. Plowing by horse or ox is very difficult.

I have watched Amish farmers plow with a horse with sweat and determination—it is hard work. Afterward, there is a waiting period when they do other things needed around the farm. Then at harvest time, though it was difficult to plant, there is now joy as the seed yields a crop to feed their families, and with more determination and joyfulness, they reap the harvest together as a family. Similarly, following God in Messiah Jesus can be difficult. With great determination, you plant the seed. The yoke you are bearing is from the Lord himself. He said, "Come to me, all *you* who labor [those who are doing, making, toiling] and are heavy laden, and I will give you rest. Take my yoke upon you and learn [to be learning, to listen, to hear (*shema*)] from Me, for I am gentle and lowly in heart, and you will find rest for your souls. For My yoke *is* easy and My burden is light" (Matt 11:28–30).

When you plow and plant with sweat and determination for the Lord ("with all your strength," Deut 6:5), there will be a waiting period as the seed grows. Then at harvest time, though it was difficult to plant, there will be joy as the seed yields a crop. And with more determination and joy, you reap the harvest together with other believers with great joy.

DAY 50

The Anchor

Before the cross became the predominant Christian symbol, the anchor was the symbol of hope and life for the early believers in the first century. As Nero was burning, torturing, and throwing Christians to the beasts, both young and old, believers would look to the anchor as a reminder of the hope they have in Jesus.

The anchor steadied a ship in the harbor or storm and was very important in navigation, thus becoming a symbol of safety.

Early Christians adopted the anchor as a symbol of hope. The Epistle of Hebrews connects the idea of hope with the symbol of the anchor: "This *hope* we have as an anchor of the soul, both sure and steadfast, and which enters the *Presence* behind the veil, where the forerunner has entered for us, *even* Jesus, having become High Priest forever according to the order of Melchizedek" (Heb 6:19-20). This hope is referring to the hope of salvation.

You can find in the cemeteries and catacombs of the early centuries epitaphs with anchors and words such as *pax tecum, pax tibi,* and *in pace* ("peace with," "peace be with you," "in peace"), speaking to their hope of heaven.

Symbolically, the hooks were associated with the catching of fish. The Greek word for fish is *ichthys*. Christians made an acrostic from this word: *Iesous Christos Theou Yios Soter* ("Jesus Christ, Son of God, Savior"). Water, where the anchor was submerged, can

THE ANCHOR

bring life or death. It also symbolized baptism, the immersion of those who believed.

Jesus said to his disciples, "Follow me, and I will make you fishers of men" (Matt 4:19). Whether by net or hook, fish are caught. "Fishers of men" refers to the disciples sharing the gospel so that people can be drawn into the kingdom through faith in the Son of God who died and rose again, shedding his blood for the remission of sin (Heb 9:22).

Jesus said, "No one can come to me unless the Father who sent me draws him; and I will raise him up on the last day" (John 6:44). To be "drawn" to Jesus is to be rescued from death to life.

The anchor symbolized that hope the early Christians desperately held on to as their lives were in peril daily.

It is good for us to remember such things. In our day, Christians often do not know their history. The early symbols, traditions, and Jewish beginnings are often overlooked.

If we don't have roots, we have no place to go and grow. Our roots must be understood and nourished for us to grow as believers in Jesus.

> Remember that you do not support the root, but the root *supports* you. (Rom 11:18)

Time is short, life is precious, and Jesus is coming soon!

About Dr. Jeff

Dr. Jeff is a dedicated expositor who provides food for thousands in the Middle East and a Bible teacher with expertise in Jewish roots of Christianity, the Middle East, and theology.

He is a pastor, humanitarian, educator, and author. His books and articles address the Jewish roots of Christianity, biblical prophecy, theology, and adventure.

He has been interviewed on various podcasts and news outlets such as *CBN* and *The Jerusalem Post*.

Dr. Jeff has an intense love for Israel and her messiah. He is motivated by intellectual curiosity, devotion to historic biblical truth, and spiritual awareness. He passionately emphasizes, "As you bless one child, it is as though you are blessing Messiah himself" (Matt 25:40).

www.israeltodayministries.org
Facebook.com/IsraelTodayMinistries
itmdrjeff@gmail.com

Bibliography

Blech, Benjamin. *More Secrets of Hebrew Words*. New Jersey: Jason Aronson, 1991.

———. *More Secrets of Hebrew Words*. New Jersey: Jason Aronson, 1993.

Buber, Martin. *The Way of Man; Ten Rungs*. New York: Citadel, 2006.

Edersheim, Alfred. *The Life and Times of Jesus the Messiah: Volume I*. Grand Rapids: Eerdmans, 1965.

———. *The Life and Times of Jesus the Messiah: Volume II*. London: Longmans, 1899.

Fruchtenbaum, Arnold G. *The Book of Genesis*. Ariel's Bible Commentary. San Antonio, TX: Ariel Ministries, 2009.

Johnson, Jeffrey D. *Divine Mysteries: Concise and Thoughtful Ancient Wisdom*. Eugene, OR: Wipf & Stock, 2019.

———. *God Was There: Genesis Chapters 1–12*. Eugene, OR: Wipf & Stock, 2005.

———. *Unlocked Treasures: Contemplative Aspects of Faith*. Eugene, OR: Wipf & Stock, 2011.

Lewis, C. S. *Letters to Malcolm, Chiefly on Prayer*. Glasgow: Collins & Sons, 1964.

Lieber, David L. *Etz Hayim: Torah and Commentary*. New York: Jewish Publication Society, 1999.

Novak, Alfons. *Hebrew Honey: A Simple and Deep Word Study of the Old Testament*. Houston, TX: Countryman, 1987.

Phillips, John. *Exploring Genesis: An Expository Commentary*. Neptune, NJ: Loizeaux, 1980.

Sarna, Nahum M. *Understanding Genesis: The Heritage of Biblical Israel*. New York: Schocken, 1970.

Scherman, Nosson. *The Stone Edition of the Chumash: The Torah, Haftaros, and Five Megillos with a Commentary Anthologized from the Rabbinic Writings*. Brooklyn: Mesorah, 2000.

Staniforth, Maxwell, trans. "The Epistle to Romans, 7." In *Early Christian Writings*, 83–89. New York: Penguin, 1968.

Trepp, Leo. *A History of the Jewish Experience*. New York: Behrman, 1973.

"Unveiling the 8 Degrees of Giving with Colel Chabad." Colel Chabad. https://colelchabad.org/eight-degrees-of-giving/.

Subject Index

Aaronic blessing, 13
Abel, 44
Abigail, 76
Abraham. *See also* Isaac; Jacob
    answering with *Hineni*, 41–42
    God's covenant with, 31, 32, 59, 85–87
    learning from Noah and Shem, 31
    recognizing angels, 7
    willingness to sacrifice Isaac, 68–70
Abram, 32, 58, 85–86, 93–94
Absalom, ix
Adam, 21–22, 55, 61, 62, 74–75
afterlife. *See* heaven
anchor, symbolism of, 130–31
angels, 7, 42, 129
ark of the covenant, 12, 18–19, 128
ascension, 77–79
Augustine, Saint, 114
Av, month of, 82–83

bartering, 108–9
Bethany (city), 24, 25
blessings, seven in Genesis, 86–87
bread, leavened, 19–20
"bride of Christ," 2
Buber, Martin, 81

challenges, life, 48–51, 71–72, 94, 116, 124

challenging times, x, 36–37
charity, 80–81. *See also* Israel Today Ministries
children
    Aaronic blessing over, 13
    affected by war of October 7, 2023, 98
    legitimacy of, 126–27
    naming, 93, 94–95
    teaching, 48, 60, 71–72, 128
chosen land, 31–33. *See also* Israel
chosen people, 58
circumstances, rising above, 125–27
covenants, 10, 31, 32, 59, 85–87
"covered [wove]," meaning of in Psalm 139, 124
creation, 9–10, 21–22, 30, 53–55, 62

David
    Abigail and, 76
    God Communicating his word through, 30–31
    parents forsaking, 71–72
    passion for God of, 29
    praising God for rescue, 35
    Psalm 139 and, 123–24
    rebellion of son of, ix
    reflecting on sovereignty of God, 34
Day of Atonement, 18–19, 34
Deborah, 76
Decalogue, 18

SUBJECT INDEX

decisions, life, 21–23
despair, 50–51, 111
disasters, 82–83, 89–90
disciples of Jesus, 117–19, 131

Eden, dust of, 21–22
Elisha, 50–51
Elohim as name of God, 9–11, 41–42
enemies, 121–22
Epistle of Hebrews, 130
Eunice, 75–76
Eve, 30, 74–75
Ezekiel, 16–17

faith
  action demonstrating, 73
  going forward in, 64–65
  overcoming obstacles and, 24–27
  strengthened through God's silence, 110–11
  testing of, 69, 86
fear, 78, 91–92
forgiveness, 19–20, 22–23, 83–84, 97. *See also* mercy
"formed," meaning of in Psalm 139, 123
free will, 8, 9–11, 22

Genesis, 9–11, 31, 86–87
gentiles, 4, 32–33, 54, 71, 87
God
  caring of, 98–100
  choices and declarations of, 30–33, 105–7
  communion and encounters with, 1–2, 15–17
  fear of, 91–92
  forgiving nature of, 19–20, 22–23, 83–84, 97
  image of, 55–56
  names of, 9–11, 41–42, 49
  noninterference of, 7–8
  praising, 34–35
  protection of, 120–22
  seeking, 28–29
  silence of, 110–11
God's kiss, 1–2
God's Smuggler (Andrew, Sherrill), 121–22
grace, 26–27, 54, 56, 110–11

Haggai (prophet), 88–90
Hallel (Psalms 113–118), 34–35
hands, raising of, 78–79
hardships and testing, 6–8, 69, 86
heaven, 30, 108–9, 112–14, 130
Hebrews, 1, 130
hiding place, 11
Hineni (here I am), 41–43
holy hush, 13
holy remembrance, 13
Holy Spirit (*Ruach HaKodesh*), 7, 19, 28, 116
holy words, 12–13
hope
  anchor as symbol of, 130–31
  cord of Rahab and, 46–47
  despair and, 50–51
  Psalm 62:5–8 and, ix
  Psalm 91 and, 6–8
  slotha and, 47
  story of Sarah and Hannah and, 47
  tragedies and, 83
  "wait" as root of Hebrew word for, 46

idolatry, 18, 77–79
Isaac, 31, 32, 59, 70
Isaiah, 16, 29, 83, 103
Israel
  as the chosen land, 31–33
  God's declaration of support of, 105–6
  as God's messenger, 35
  inclusion of Gentiles into, 71
  olive tree as symbol of, 115–16

SUBJECT INDEX

Israel Today Ministries (ITM), ix–x, 73, 95, 109
Israeli border wall, 24–27

Jacob, 30–31, 94
James the Just (brother of Jesus), 73, 108–9
Jephthah, 125–27
Jeremiah, 15–17
Jerusalem, 38–40, 57–59
Jesus
  being for all nations, 35
  disciples of, 117–19, 131
  on enemies, 121
  first miracle of, 52–54
  on forgiveness of sin, 4
  as God, 117–19
  heaven promised by, 112, 113
  journey of those following, 26–27
  meaning of name of, 118–19
  mission to humanity from, 60
  on tribulation and testing, 6
  worship received by, 66–67
Job, 118–19
John, 52–54, 81, 112, 113, 117
Jonah, 97
Jubilee, xi
Judaism. *See also* Talmud; Ten Commandments; *specific holidays*
  faith in Messiah Yeshua, 54, 116
  God's name unspeakable in, 10
  the Messiah and, 2
  the *mikvah*, 78
  Shema prayer and, 48, 128–29
  on worship of a human, 118

Lazarus (brother of Mary and Martha), 24, 26, 112
Lois, 75–76
"longsuffering." *See* patience
love (*ahav*), 14, 29, 68–70

Maimonides, Moses, 80
Martha (sister of Mary and Lazarus), 24, 67, 112
Mary (mother of Jesus), 66
Mary (sister of Martha and Lazarus), 24, 67
mercy, 10, 18, 19–20, 22–23, 56. *See also* forgiveness
Messiah. *See also* Jesus
  Communion and, 13
  goodness from, 36–37
  Israel and, 31
  Jerusalem and, 38
  Jews awaiting, 2
  message of hope in, 99–100
  transformation through, 94
mikvah (Jewish ritual bath), 78
miracles, 21, 47, 50–54, 110, 123–24
Moriah, 68–69
Moses
  Genesis and, 21
  God speaking face-to-face with, 1
  God's patience and, 61, 63
  Hineni and, 42–43
  Mt. Sinai ascension, 18–19
  parting the Red Sea, 64
  revelation upon receiving the Torah, 53
  on Satan, 3
Muslim Jihadists, 26
"my inward parts," meaning of in Psalm 139, 123–24

Nabal, 76
names, 93–95
Noah, 31, 64
nomadic peoples, 31

Obadiah, wife of, 50–51
obedience, 89
olive tree, symbolism of, 115–16

SUBJECT INDEX

Palestine, 25
parents, 71–72, 126–27
Passover, 19–20, 96–97
patience, 61–63
Paul, 3, 74, 94, 116, 119
peace (*shalom*), x, 3–8, 64–65, 130
Pentecost. *See* Shavuot (Pentecost)
Peseach Sheni (Second Passover), 96
Peter
    name of, 94
    passion for God of, 28, 29
    role of in Shavuot (Pentecost), 19
    sermon in the temple, 2
    trust in Jesus of, 118
prayers
    for enemies, 121
    Hebrew and Yiddish words for, 102
    importance of, 101–4
    morning, 13, 48–49
    practice of, 103–4
    Shema, 48, 128–29
problems, 88–90
prophecy, living word of, 1–2
Puah, 75
purpose, discovering, 128–29

Rahab, 46–47
raising of hands, symbolism of, 36
Rebekah, 70
Red Sea, parting of, 64
remembrance, holy, 13
repentance (*teshuvah*), 96–97
restoration, 83–84

sacrifices, 20, 68–70
Sarah, 31, 47, 59
Satan, 3, 66
Scripture, provocation toward, 4–5
scroll of mysteries and truths, 16–17
Second Passover, 96
security, ix, 6–8

self, preoccupation with, 36–37
seraphim, 16
Shabbat, 13
Shavuot, 18–20
Shem, 31
Shema prayer, 48, 128–29
Shiprah, 75
Shulamite, 1, 62
silence, God's, 110–11
sin
    "fear of the Lord" and, 91–92
    forgiveness of, 10, 13, 20
    Jesus on forgiveness of, 4
    leaven as a type of, 19
    purification of Isaiah of, 16
Solomon, 62, 77
"Song of Plagues," 6–8
Song of Songs, the Greatest Lover (Johnson), 2
suffering, 116
swearing falsely, 108

Talmud, 6, 21, 28, 80–81
Ten Commandments, 18–20, 71–72
testing. *See* hardships and testing
Tetragrammaton, 10
Timothy, 75–76
Torah, 12, 52–53, 85, 128, 129

vanity (*hevel*), 44–45

waiting, 46–47
"womb," meaning of in Psalm 139, 124
women, 74–76. *See also specific women*
words, holy, 12–13
words to remember, 57–60
worship, authentic, 36–37

YHVH Elohim, 10, 11
Yom Kippur, 18–19. *See also* Israel Today Ministries

Scripture Index

OLD TESTAMENT

Genesis

	9
1	9, 54, 94
1:1–25	21
1:9–13	52
1:10	52
1:12	52
1:17	22
1:19—2:11	52
1:26	22
1:27	55
2	9, 10
2:7	21, 22, 62
2:23	74
3	10
12:1	58
12:1–3	31, 32, 33, 35
12:2–3	85, 86
12:3	58
13:15–17	32
15:18	31
17:1–8	85
17:5	94
17:7	32
17:7–8	59
17:8	32
17:18–19	59
17:19	32
18	7
18:25	111
22	77
22:1	41, 42
22:2	68
22:3	41, 69
22:4	41, 69
22:5	69
22:8	41
22:9	41
22:11	42
22:12	42, 70
22:13	70
22:14	42, 70
22:17	85
24:67	70
26:3–4	86
27:28–29	86
31:45–49	126
32:28	30, 94
35:9–15	32

Exodus

1:15–22	75
3:1–4	42
3:5	68
3:6	42
3:7	42
14:13	118
14:13–15	64

Exodus (continued)

19	54
19:16	53
19–32	18
24:7	129
31	55
32	61
32:19	18
32:20	18
32:30	18
32:34	18
33	61
33:11	1, 61
33:18–23	62
34:2	18
34:6	63
34:8	63
34:28	18

Leviticus

25	xi
25:23	59

Numbers

6:24–26	13, 86
9:1–14	96
13	82

Deuteronomy

5:24	53
6:1–9	128
6:4	x, 128
6:4–5	59
6:4–9	48
6:5	129
6:6–7	60
6:7	128
7:6	58
8:3	2
9:9–11	18
9:25	18
10:1–5	18
10:17	3
18:15	2
18:18	2
18:19	2
24:20	115

Joshua

2:18	47

Judges

10:16	98
11	125
11:1	125, 126
11:1–11	125
11:2	125, 127
11:3	125, 127
11:4	125
11:4–6	127
11:5	126
11:6	126
11:7	126
11:7–11	127
11:8	126
11:9	126
11:10	126
11:11	126
11:29	127

1 Samuel

25	76
25:25	94

2 Kings

4	50
4:2–7	50

1 Chronicles

16:36	111
21	77

SCRIPTURE INDEX

2 Chronicles

3	77
7:14	83

Job

9:8–11	119
42:1–2	27

Psalms

	11, 13
2:12	2
5	77
15	77
15:1	78
18:1–2	11
19:1	21, 30, 110
24	77
24:1	77
24:3	37, 78
24:3–5	77
24:3–6	77
24:4	37, 78
24:5	79
27:10–11	72
30:5	100
32:7	11
40:3	104
40:17	3, 23, 106
48	39
48:12–13	60
62:5	46
63:1–3	28
63:2–3	29
71:5	47
91	6, 7, 116
91:1	56
91:1–4	56
91:3–8	120
91:4	56
94:22	11
103:20	129
113	34
113–118	34
114	34
115	35
116	35
117	35
118	35
118:5	35
118:9	35
118:29	35
119:89–90	31
122:1	37, 78
122:6	57
130:5	46
137:5	38
138:2	31
139	72, 123
139:13	123
139:13–17	22
147:4	94

Proverbs

8:17	29
9:10	91
14:26–27	92
22:4	91

Ecclesiastes

	44
1:2	44

Song of Solomon

	2
1:2	1, 62

Isaiah

	16
2:4	83
6	92
6:1	29
6:5	29, 37, 78
6:6	16
6:7	16
11:1	39

SCRIPTURE INDEX

Isaiah (continued)

11:3	91
11:12	39
14:1–2	32
17:6	115
33:14	78
33:15	78
40:31	111
41:1–7	105
41:8	105
41:9	105
41:10–12	106
41:13	6, 23, 49, 97, 105, 106
41–45	106
42:1	87
42:6	87
43:5–11	39
43:10	35
43:10–11	58
44:28—45:4	105
49:5	87
49:6	87
49:22	33
52:9	83
60:15	83
65:18	83
65:19	83
66:1	77

Jeremiah

1:9	15
31:20	98
32:37	39
33:3	104

Lamentations

3	xi, 22
3:20–24	97
3:22	23, 124
3:23	23, 124

Ezekiel

	16
3	16
5:5	58
37:21	39
37:22	39

Hosea

11:8	99

Amos

9:11	87
9:12	87
9:13	54
9:13–15	39

Jonah

1:4	97
3:1	97, 127

Haggai

1:5–6	88
1:7–8	89
1:9–11	89
1:12–13	89
2:3	89
2:4	90
2:5	90
2:6–9	90
2:15–19	90

Zechariah

2:8	58
14	38

RABBINIC WORKS

Mishnah

Sanhedrin 4:5	21

SCRIPTURE INDEX

Talmud

Bava Batra 14b — 19
"Song of Plagues" (Shev Shema'tata) 15b — 6

Yerushalmi Talmud

4:9 — 21

NEW TESTAMENT

Matthew

Reference	Page
2:11	66
4:10	66
4:19	131
5:33–37	108
5:44	121
9:36	99
11:28–30	129
14:28	118
14:32	118
14:33	66, 118
18:18–20	60
20:28	7
23:29	54
24:45–47	113
25:20–23	113
25:40	57, 133
26:10	67
26:63	108
26:64	108
28:9	66

Mark

Reference	Page
6:48	118
14:33	69

Luke

Reference	Page
1:37	110
2:32	54
7:12–13	99
10:42	67
11:1	47
14:15–24	112–13
14:25–35	116
15:20	63
18:15–17	110
19:15–19	113
20:21	4
22:42	69
22:44	69
23:34	63
24:52	67

John

Reference	Page
1:1	117
1:3	53
1:14	54, 117
2	51, 52, 54
2:1	52
2:1–10	52
2:3	53
2:6	53
2:7	53
2:8–10	53
3:16	68
4:22	35
5:17	113
6:20	118
6:21	118
6:37	112
6:39	112
6:44	131
6:63	57
8:56	70
8:58	54
9:38	66
10:27	2
10:30	67
11:23	112
11:25–26	112
11:33–36	99
13	7
14:1–3	112
14:6	60
14:12	113

John (continued)

15:14	106
15:16	106
16:5–15	116
16:33	8

Acts

2	19
3	2
11:26	94
17:25	110

Romans

5:20	54
8:24–25	111
8:25	47
8:26–27	111
8:28–39	111
8:35–39	7
11	71
11:5	84
11:13	4
11:14	4
11:18	131
11:33	128
13	106
16:1	74
16:3	74
16:6	74
16:7	74
16:12	74
16:13	74
16:15	74
16:20	3

1 Corinthians

1:11	74
2:9	112
6:19–20	7
13:12	113
15:52	70
15:54	113
15:57	113
16:19	74

2 Corinthians

1:23	108
5:17	110
5:21	36

Galatians

3:29	35
5:22	116
5:22–23	73
5:23	116

Ephesians

1:5–7	56
1:6–7	56
2	71
2:1–14	20
3	71
5:21	91

Philippians

1:29	116
2:10	67
3:10	116
4:2	74
4:5–7	x

Colossians

1:16	119
2	30
4:15	74

2 Timothy

3:12	116
3:14	75
3:15	76
4:19	74
4:20	74

Philemon

2	74

Hebrews 130

1:1	1
1:2	1
6:19–20	130
9:22	131
11:1	110, 111
11:6	110
11:17–19	69
12:14	110
13:5	111
13:5–6	6

James

2:18	73
5:12	109

1 Peter

3:4	75
3:5	75
5:10	116

2 Peter

1:16	28
1:16–21	29
1:18	28
1:20–21	28

1 John

1:8–10	110
1:9	83
2:2	20
3:2	112
3:10	81
4:4	110

Revelation

5:14	67
14:13	113
21:3–4	113

EARLY CHRISTIAN WRITINGS

Augustine

City of God

504	114n1

www.ingramcontent.com/pod-product-compliance
Lightning Source LLC
Chambersburg PA
CBHW071608170426
43196CB00034B/2239